The Great Interior Design Challenge

Foreword by Tom Dyckhoff

PAVILION

WHERE TO START

Contents

THE BIG PICTURE

DECORATING DETAILS

Foreword

On *The Great Interior Design Challenge* I had the best job of all. I didn't have to spend hours slaving over a jigsaw like our contestants, or dispensing sharp-eyed critical advice like our judges. I got to show people their new room – to walk through the door with them and reveal their previously cluttered living room, creaky kitchen or battered bedroom transformed by our skilful amateur designers into a magnificent new incarnation.

On occasion there was the odd awkward silence; we had our disappointments. But mostly the homeowners' wide eyes and dropped jaws signalled amazement, a splash of relief and a genuine love for what their amateur designers had achieved in their home so quickly, so creatively and with such little money. And yes, there were tears. This was their home, after all. And these were people who, for instance, hadn't changed a room in three decades because it contained memories of a life now past, or who were working every hour possible to pay the mortgage and just needed one peaceful spot in the home to retreat to at the end of a day, or who'd left behind a life of homelessness and needed help to work out what exactly 'being at home' meant. These were people who knew exactly how important home was to them, and I got to see it, first hand. What a privilege.

You see, interior design is a serious business: where we put the sofa, what colour we paint the walls – it all matters. Some might consider it a frivolous thing, a preoccupation with cushions, curtains, the storage of DVDs and the correct position of ornaments somehow unimportant. Not a bit of it. At its best, the British home – whether a classic terraced house, a 1930s semi or a stately home – can be a design classic, even a work of art, both outside and in.

Our homes, though, are so much more than that. They are the most important spaces, the most important kind of architecture, we shall ever experience. Nobody knows our homes better than we do. We form deep, intimate relationships with every patch of the sofa we sit on every night watching the TV. I could walk blindfolded round my home and barely stub my toes. I know every inch. Behind our front doors is where we are most

ourselves, where we can be who we really are, where we don't have to put on a public face, but can love and laugh and argue with the people closest to us. Our homes are where we do the important big things and important little things of life. And whether we choose to decorate them like Liberace or Frank Gallagher, our interior design, or lack of it, can't help but express who we are and who we want to be.

Sometimes, though, we can get in a rut. Our homes are not how we would like them to be; they get cluttered with stuff, with knick-knacks and books and consoles and electronic wires and so on. We moan about the dodgy shelving system we threw up one Sunday afternoon, clinging onto the wall on a wing and a prayer. We haven't got time to paint the living room. We haven't got the money. We haven't got the headspace. And it drives us crazy. Every time we walk in, the mess, the wrongness of the room nags at us as if we are wearing shoes just that little bit too small.

Which is where creative thinking – like that of our 24 amateur designers – comes in. We all have a friend who has an eye for interior design. What's been incredible on *The Great Interior Design Challenge* has been watching those people transform into professionals, liaising with their clients, dealing with their problems and letting their creative brains rip. They have a gift.

This book shares that gift. It contains the accumulated wisdom of our 24 amateur designers and the homes and households they transformed. It shows you how to work with, or creatively against, the architectural style of your home, how to choose the right paint colours, how to sand wooden floorboards – all the practical and creative stuff. But, most importantly of all, it will help you get out of the rut. It will finally allow your home – and you – to be who you really want to be. And – even better – you can finally get that dodgy shelving system fixed, once and for all.

Tom Dyckhoff

Where to start

Whether you are designing your entire home from scratch or simply refreshing a single room, a little time spent on thoughtful planning will really pay off. In this section, we will help you work out what personal style suits you best and assist you in your choice of colours and patterns. We will show you how to pull all your ideas together, plan your work and draw up a budget – and even give you ideas for when to do it yourself (safely, of course) or when and how to work with a professional.

Find your style

The way you design your home says just as much about you as the clothes you wear. This is your space: as well as being perfectly suited to your lifestyle, it should look beautiful and make you feel good, too.

What is your interior style? Perhaps you can give a snappy, one-word answer straight away. Perhaps you have to think for a while. Or maybe you just don't know. Finding a style is an opportunity to explore the way in which you want to live. It is not about fitting into a set of rules, but about exploring what works best for you, what suits the structure of your home, and what elements will bring you happiness on a daily basis.

The best way to start is by thinking about who lives in the house and how you use it. Which rooms do you spend most time in, and at what times of day? Where do you need spaces that are light and bright, and what areas can be cosy and intimate? Are you formal, or more relaxed? How tidy are you (be honest)? Consider the architecture of your home, and its location, too – an Art Deco seaside home suits a different style to, say, a Georgian townhouse, while a rural cottage lends itself to yet another look.

Architecture aside, however, you should also think about your own taste and personality. When you flick through a book or magazine, watch a television programme or walk round the shops, what styles appeal the most? Do you yearn for a romantic retreat, full of ornaments and pretty colours, or hanker after a tough, industrial look in minimal black and grey? Are you thoroughly modern, retro-obsessed or a lover of antiques and period details? Perhaps you are inspired by foreign travels or a special place that you once visited. Do not worry: this is not a test, and you can't get the answers wrong. Relax and enjoy the process, because once you start to define your style you are on the way to creating a unique vision of how you want to live.

Period Details

If you are lucky enough to live in an older home with original architectural details, it is worth ensuring that they are restored to their full glory, and complemented by a well-chosen decorative scheme. While an exact replica of a particular period style may be slightly over the top, a few retro or antique pieces could be just the thing to enhance the overall character of your home. On the other hand, you may wish to contrast your period details with ultra-modern furniture. Either way, finding out about the history of your home is always a rewarding endeavour, and will stand you in good stead when you are making design decisions.

→ A fabulous original feature:
from the mid-1880s, cast-iron
fireplaces adorned with elaborate,
colourful tiles were becoming
highly fashionable.

Period character

Georgian sash windows

Fashionable houses featured double-hung sash windows. After 1709 they were inset to prevent fire spreading.

Regency ironwork

Cast-iron features in classically inspired geometric forms and floral designs were common.

Georgian internal door

A six-panel door such as this, featuring a moulded doorcase, is typical of a late Georgian property.

Georgian cornice

The acanthus leaf pattern was hugely popular in the late Georgian period.

Victorian internal door

A four-panelled, wooden door like this is a type commonly found in modest Victorian houses.

Victorian ceiling rose

Ornate ceiling roses make a wonderful feature in many Victorian homes.

Victorian fireplace

From the late 1850s, cast-iron fireplaces were mass-produced, usually with ornamental tiled panels.

Victorian letterbox

Letterboxes became common after the introduction of the Penny Post in 1840. This one is also a knocker.

Edwardian balusters

New technology made square-cut shapes such as these less expensive to produce.

Edwardian fireplace

Stained pine has replaced Victorian dark oak for this Tudor-style surround. Patterned tiles were also popular.

1930s window

Long metal windows with two opening casements and fixed central sections were common in 1930s modern houses.

1930s door

Doors often combined metal and glass, and the sunray motif is typical of the period.

Global influences

When it comes to design inspiration, we literally have a whole world of styles from which to choose.

For many people, decorating in a global style means finding a way to incorporate a special piece brought back from a trip abroad – an item of furniture, a colourful rug or a length of unusual fabric – into an overall scheme. Or it could simply be the desire to evoke the atmosphere of a region by choosing specific colours, patterns and textures. This is an opportunity to search auctions, antiques and charity shops and jumble sales for interesting pieces, or spend foreign holidays in souks and flea markets, workshops and rug shops,

soaking up the atmosphere in order to replicate it back home. Even if you are on a tight budget, just one or two inexpensive pieces can create a eye-catching display.

When decorating with a global perspective, you can mix and match as much as you like. Just as historical styles do not begin and end at exact times, so global styles tend not to stop at man-made political boundaries. By exploring the wealth of beautiful crafts and furnishings from around the world, you can create your own individual and appealing look.

Scandinavian

▶ Light, bright and airy.

▶ Pale colours with dashes of heartening red, green, yellow and mid-blue.

▶ Sheer and checked fabrics.

▶ Painted wooden furniture.

▶ Curly metal chandeliers and mirror-backed sconces.

Classic French

▶ Smart and sophisticated.

▶ Glass chandeliers, curly metalwork and oversized mirrors.

▶ Rich fabrics with arabesque patterns of ribbons, garlands and swags.

▶ Neutral colours such as grey, taupe and eau de nil, combined with stronger shades such as burgundy and navy.

Indian

- ▶ Relaxed, comfortable and eclectic.

- ▶ Saturated shades, including pink, crimson, orange, saffron, lime and purple.

- ▶ Luscious fabrics, sometimes including metal threads.

- ▶ Dark wood furniture, embellished with brass.

- ▶ Beaten metal, earthenware and wooden lattice-work accessories.

- ▶ Intricate patterns, especially featuring the boteh, the teardrop shape featured in paisley.

Mediterranean

- ▶ Simple, vibrant and informal.

- ▶ Vivid colours, including earthy terracottas, sunny yellows and geranium reds.

- ▶ Hand-crafted furnishings.

- ▶ Multicoloured, flat-woven rugs.

- ▶ Striped, checked and floral fabrics.

North African

- ▶ Richly decorative and sensual.

- ▶ Geometric and floral patterns.

- ▶ Warm colours such as mustard, ruby, saffron, emerald and orange.

- ▶ Intricate and colourful tilework.

- ▶ Floor cushions and bolsters.

The modern approach

Do you yearn for simplicity or adore a cosy, colourful look? Now is the time to express your individuality.

If you don't plan to include historical or global references into your decorating scheme, you may wonder just what is your style. Well, the answer is that the modern home can be anything you want it to be – pared-down and minimal, rustic and natural, pretty and nostalgic – but above all, it should be your vision, your look, your very own style.

No matter what your type of property, or where you live, pulling together a modern look that suits you perfectly is not necessarily difficult, time-consuming or expensive – it may simply be a question of re-thinking what goes where, giving a lick of paint to one or two key pieces, and adding some inexpensive accessories. The aim is to create an impression of visual coherence so it all just feels 'right'. Think about colours, patterns, textures, furniture, fabrics and lighting (they all come later in this book). There are plenty of styles to choose from, all of them a pleasure to live with and easy on the eye. Now it's up to you.

Simple

▶ Fuss-free and functional.

▶ Off-whites combined with stronger colours.

▶ Natural materials – wood, slate, wicker, wool and cotton.

▶ Simple furniture in timeless shapes.

▶ Plain and striped fabrics; plain white tiles.

▶ Tongue-and-groove panelling on walls.

Industrial

▶ Minimal yet rugged.

▶ Monochrome colours, especially black, white and grey.

▶ Brick, concrete, metal and glass.

▶ Sleek furniture with simple outlines.

▶ Salvaged lighting.

Country

- ▶ Comfortable, charming and timeless.
- ▶ Floral fabrics for soft furnishings.
- ▶ The colours of a country garden.
- ▶ A farmhouse kitchen (or at least a wooden dresser to give a country flavour).
- ▶ Traditional crockery such as blue-and-white striped or spongeware.
- ▶ Block-printed wallpapers.
- ▶ Baskets, Lloyd Loom furniture and cosy throws on beds, chairs and sofas.

Romantic

- ▶ Floaty and feminine.
- ▶ Droplet chandeliers and etched glass.
- ▶ Lace and sheer fabrics.
- ▶ Pale colours and faded patterns.
- ▶ Delicate metal furniture.
- ▶ Vintage teacups, glass and picture frames.

Retro

- ▶ Individual and eye-catching.
- ▶ Statement pieces from past eras.
- ▶ Plastic kitsch or mid-century modern cool.
- ▶ Lava lamps, geometric fabric and coloured glass.
- ▶ Iconic furniture and/or inexpensive and interesting finds.

Your style – making it work

You don't need deep pockets to create a great interior, just some time, effort and a little thoughtful ingenuity.

In real life, very few of us live in the sort of homes one sees in magazines or on the TV. Unless you have spent a fortune and acquired all of your furniture in one go, you're likely to have an assortment of things that don't quite match – a dining table inherited from grandparents, an antique bookshelf bought at auction, a nice bed from a high-street store, a retro chair you found in a charity shop. It can be hard to see how such diverse items can be put together to create a coherent decorative scheme. But with some basic principles you will soon be able to combine old and new, antique and modern, vintage and contemporary with aplomb – and in a way that suits both your style and your budget.

A ten-point plan for mix-and-match interiors

1 Assess your furniture and how it works in each room. What goes well together and what sticks out like a sore thumb?

2 Move furniture around, sell or give it away as appropriate. Start looking everywhere for items you are short of – from the high street to auction houses, antiques shops to car boot sales.

3 Try to limit the variation in heights of furnishings – tops of bookcases, sofas, tables and so on. The room will appear more unified.

④ Scale is important. A pair of sofas, for example, works best if they are in proportion rather than one being tall and overstuffed and the other low and lean.

⑤ Choose timeless, well-made designs. It doesn't matter what period they come from (within reason): they will work well with other pieces.

⑥ Transform pieces that don't suit your scheme. A lick of paint or a new loose cover can work wonders.

⑦ Co-ordinate colours and patterns and create a pleasing variety of textures.

⑧ Keep flooring simple: this provides a calm backdrop for everything else.

⑨ Avoid too many 'star' pieces that distract the eye. One or two wow-factor items are enough.

⑩ Keep experimenting – you may not get it right first time, but it's worth trying again. 'If in doubt, take it out' is a good rule of thumb.

Where to find style inspiration

Inspiration is all around us, but everyone needs a little nudge in the right direction from time to time. Here are just a few ideas.

▶ Decorating and furniture showrooms

▶ Markets

▶ Books, magazines and catalogues

▶ The architecture and history of your home

▶ Other people's houses

▶ Films and TV programmes

▶ Shops, restaurants and hotels

▶ Art galleries and museums

▶ The world around you – rural or urban

▶ Your own wardrobe

▶ Blogs and digital magazines

▶ A favourite piece of furniture that you already own

FURNITURE
p.180

Hopton's Almshouses
Southwark 1749

Almshouses, or homes for those in need, can be traced back to the 10th century. Before the days of state provision for the poor, wealthy individuals would leave money in their wills to establish almshouses that were named after them, hoping for rewards in heaven in return. They often catered for a certain type of person – usually elderly, and sometimes from a specific trade.

Hopton's Almshouses were built thanks to the legacy of Charles Hopton, who died in 1730 in Westminster, London. By 1749, 26 one-up, one-down houses had been built on a patch of land next to what is now Blackfriars Bridge – then a quiet, rural area. The first almsmen, mostly retired fishermen and boatmen, moved into their homes in 1752. The tenants had to adhere to a rule book that included no swearing or skipping church.

For 200 years the houses remained unchanged, although the first gas lamp was installed in 1830, and electricity arrived in 1934 – around the same time as a bathroom, library and rest room. Major refurbishments took place in the 1950s (when indoor plumbing was introduced) and the 1980s; now there are 20 one-bedroom houses and flats. Outside, however, they have barely changed from when Hopton's was built more than 260 years ago.

▶ Hopton's is built to a typical almshouse plan: a three-sided square around a garden – providing a sense of safety and security without isolating the residents from the outside world.

▶ Today more than 35,000 people live in almshouses all around the UK, many of them in the hearts of villages, towns and cities.

▶ The rooms at Hopton's would originally have been unfurnished. Occupants had to bring their own furniture, which was retained when they either died or were thrown out – so that, eventually, the interiors of the houses encompassed a variety of styles and designs.

▶ Almshouses are basic, rustic and hardwearing, built for function rather than form – but a few features date them to the middle of the Georgian period, including the arched window shapes and the large sash windows with many small panes of glass. Originally, they had 'boarded' doors, which would have been cheaper to produce and more durable than panelled ones, and a 'dog leg' staircase in the corner of the room, designed to be as compact as possible. Their fireplaces (now bricked up) would once have doubled as a stove and hob.

▶ The deep green of the front doors at Hopton's was a popular colour for rural houses in Georgian England.

← Prior to renovations in the 1950s the living rooms would have looked this; the dog leg staircase in the corner was designed to keep the stairs as compact as possible.

→ Hopton's is now surrounded by modern London.

Work, Rest & Play

A fresh, clean look, plenty of useful storage and clever references to the owner's passions transformed this small living room into an attractive, multi-functional space.

BRIEF

Keen cyclist and traveller Nigel wanted a comfortable, light and inviting living room that could accommodate a variety of uses: relaxing and watching television, eating and, crucially, building and repairing bicycles. Accessible storage for small components was another requirement, as was some sort of rack system for wheel rims. Nigel also asked for new curtains or blinds (he hated his nets), a new ceiling light to replace his dated wooden one, splashes of warm colour and, ideally, a wooden floor. He wanted to keep the world map on the wall and a wicker chair that was perfect for his bad back.

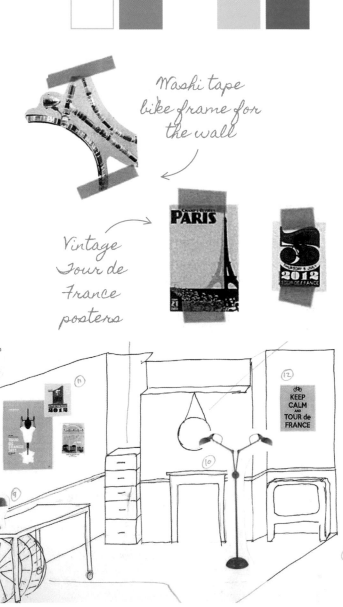

Washi tape bike frame for the wall

Vintage Tour de France posters

BEFORE

→ The designer's proposal shows a desk with room for storing bike wheels beneath; storage is also incorporated into the alcoves each side of the reinstated fireplace. The walls feature references to the cycling that Nigel loves.

↓ Folding chairs and a desk on castors make the most of a small space; Nigel's world map allows him to plot his next cycling adventure.

▶ A coat of white paint gives the room a clean, bright and fresh look, and creates a feeling of space. A 'racing' stripe in yellow adds definition but was tricky to pull off.

▶ Sturdy shelves for storing wheel rims were installed in the alcove on one side of the fireplace, with a storage tower below for small components. In the other alcove Nigel's storage unit has been used as a TV stand.

▶ The old patterned carpet was taken up and the floorboards were sanded and varnished. This provides an easy-clean surface with timeless good looks.

▶ The simple wooden desk, which is on castors so it can be moved easily, doubles as a work space/dining table. Folding chairs can be tucked out of the way when necessary.

▶ The designer has brightened up the clean work and living space with brightly coloured artwork, much of it original.

AFTER

HOW TO SAND FLOORBOARDS
p.115

DESIGN HIGHLIGHT

↓ The designer created an ingenious pendant light made from a cycle wheel and went to the trouble of sourcing a giant light bulb to fit.

→↘ More original art has been created using wire, while a cork wall map provides somewhere to pin mementoes.

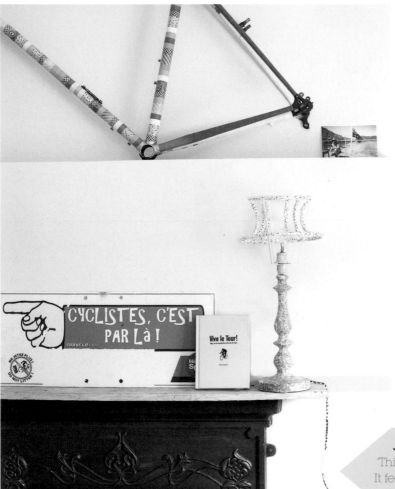

→ In keeping with the pared-down feel of the room, the curtains have been replaced with functional blinds.

→ Hand-printed cushion covers have been used to brighten up plain chairs.

JUDGE'S VIEW

'This room is quirky, creative and arty. It feels slightly like being in a very nice shop.'

CASE STUDY Clutter-free & Modern

Clever colours, well thought-out storage and careful placement of furniture have been brought together in a bold and striking scheme.

BRIEF

Deborah wanted a living room that felt homely, comfortable and welcoming: a space for her and her son to relax in, but also somewhere to entertain friends. She was feeling overwhelmed by clutter and wanted some help to clear it out and also to find storage solutions. She liked the idea of a Moroccan theme so she could incorporate some recently acquired pieces of furniture. She had worked hard to restore the parquet floor, but thought rugs might help break up the room.

BEFORE

Bold pattern and punched metal pendants

Leather pouffes

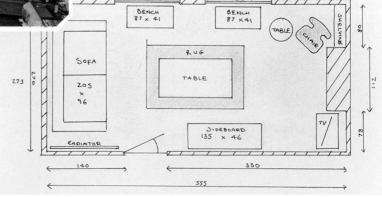

→ The designer's comprehensive mood board clearly shows her ideas for flooring and furnishings as well as colour swatches and a floor plan.

JUDGE'S VIEW
The design is very
together, very professional,
very coherent. It's calm,
tasteful, elegant and
a place you'd
like to be.'

▶ Cool, pale colours help to maximise the feeling of space in a narrow room.

▶ Storage has been added in the form of shelving on one side of the fireplace.

▶ Low level seating at the same height as the coffee table means that Deborah can entertain without needing a dining table.

▶ So as not to overpower the room, the designer has included stylish elements of Moroccan design: the rug, a painted mirror, a leather pouffe and striking pendant lamp shade, brightly-coloured cushions and groups of candles.

→ The designer has made use of Deborah's existing artwork and has grouped mounted photographs to good effect.

↓ Deborah's old wooden sideboard has been upcycled and painted red. Bright colours need to be applied carefully to achieve a professional finish.

AFTER

↑ The rug makes the room feel more comfortable as well as complementing the Moroccan theme with a striking design.

USING PATTERN
p.38

CASE STUDY | A Chintz-free Zone

A client with a strong sense of style offered an opportunity as well as a challenge for the designer of this living/working/kitchen space.

BRIEF

Jazz musician Shamus used to work as a gardener at Hopton's and he moved in five years ago. His room comprised three elements; kitchen, dining/living and work place. He wanted an 'old fashioned' look and was keen to incorporate in the design his many lovely pieces of furniture, including dining chairs and a desk, as well as an eclectic mix of antiques – such as his old black telephone, brass oil lamps, mantle clocks and other interesting trinkets. Shamus loved the 1940s film-noir style, especially the movie *Casablanca*, and many of his ornaments fit in with this era. He wanted to avoid chintz or chandeliers.

BEFORE

→ The designer's proposal shows detailed colour swatches and a wide selection of design inspirations but lacks a floor plan – essential when designing a multi-purpose room.

Fretwork screens

The film Casablanca was a key inspiration

Deep, rich colours and Morrocan tea gasses

↓ Replacement
cupboard doors give
the kitchen a whole
new look.

AFTER

▶ The walls were washed with sugar soap to remove tobacco stains.

▶ Colour has been used to great effect: the greens are calming, while the cool grey has been warmed by the wooden furniture. The grey also prevents the wood from looking too orange.

▶ The lattice-work cupboard fronts echo the north African, Casablanca theme.

▶ New cupboard doors and handles have given Shamus the Shaker-style kitchen he wanted.

▶ The floor-to-ceiling shelving in the alcove is a good use of space.

▶ The designer has successfully reinvigorated furniture by careful sanding and treating with linseed oil.

▶ A cork floor gives the room a warm feel and is suitable for the room's many uses.

↑ Shamus's oil lamps
were incorporated into
the design.

TYPES OF
FLOORING p.113

← Shamus's telephone and other vintage collectibles take pride of place.

↓ Moroccan-style cupboard doors conceal Shamus's music equipment.

← Adjustable bookshelves span the alcove beside the old chimney breast.

JUDGE'S VIEW
'The colours work extremely well. The greens are calming and the grey helps the room seem bigger.'

Project

At the almshouses the designers were each given a basic lamp base and shade to upcycle however they liked. If you want to update a lampshade, covering it with fabric is both quick and easy.

A painted base and découpage.

A deconstructed lamp.

A musical collage.

HOW TO COVER A LAMPSHADE

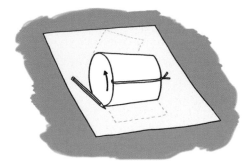

1 To make a template tie a length of wool around the shade. Place on its side on some newspaper with the wool touching the paper. Mark this point and roll the shade and the wool across the paper, marking its path top and bottom until you have gone through 360°. Add 1cm (⅜in) around your finished shape and cut out.

2 Place the template on the right side of the fabric and cut out. With the fabric right side down, turn up 1cm (⅜in) along both long edges and one short edge and press. Place the fabric over the shade, lining up the seams.

3 Using spray fabric adhesive, and following the manufacturer's instructions, spray along the unpressed edge and then smooth the pressed edge over the top for a neat finish. Spray the seam allowance along top and bottom edges of the fabric and carefully fold down over the shade. Then use fire-retardant spray over the entire shade according to the manufacturer's instructions.

Colour

It's time to get colour-confident, because nothing adds more character to a room than an inspired choice of hues.

Colour can be mellow and muted or thrilling and dynamic – and it affects us in a powerful way. Our strong response to colour stems from millions of years of evolution, in which different hues served as vital indicators of danger or safety: poisonous yellow berries or lush green fields, for example.

Colour can uplift or depress us, and can even produce a physical reaction: bright red induces a rapid heartbeat and is an appetite stimulant, while soft blue causes the body to produce calming chemicals. Colour is also symbolic: red for anger, white for purity, yellow for cowardice, and so on. And, of course, we each have our own feelings about colour, so that one person's exciting, energising room is another's nightmare of brash, clashing shades. Colour is often the key to the overall look and feel of a room: it is an incredibly versatile, effective and satisfying tool. And, of course, our colour choices are as individual as we are, which is exactly why colour can be so creative.

↑ In this room a bright yellow wall is balanced by a neutral one so that the effect is not overwelming.

Colour know-how

▶ Use pale, 'cool' colours (such as blues and greens) to make small rooms appear bigger. Darker, warmer colours (for instance red and terracotta) make large spaces seem cosier.

▶ Don't know where to start with paint colours? Buy some sample pots and paint sheets of white card with at least two coats of your chosen colours and tape them up around the room. Watch how they change in different lights – for example, what might look like a lovely purple in daylight is almost black at night.

▶ A tungsten light bulb makes colours much more yellow, while halogen is more blue; intense sunlight makes colours paler, but a setting sun warms them up.

▶ Take care with colours that are on the borderline between two different shades: they can change unexpectedly in different light conditions.

▶ Stand in the hall or on the landing – can you see a number of different rooms at once? Choose co-ordinating colours so that they link together.

▶ Always use the correct shade of undercoat for your chosen colour of paint – it can affect the way it looks.

▶ Take inspiration from paint colour cards, fabric books and decorating websites: they have put beautiful schemes together so you don't have to.

↖ Cool grey-blue walls are warmed by a wooden floor and sunny yellow chairs.

← Emerald green paint transforms a set of shelves into an eye-catching feature.

Versatile neutrals

Neutral colours are the little black dresses of interior design: easy to use, versatile and always good looking.

Understated, calm and inviting, neutral colours are timelessly fashionable and eternally appealing. They link rooms harmoniously, look good in small or large spaces and provide the perfect backdrop for works of art or collections.

There is only one drawback. Let's face it: neutrals can be a little dull. Even though they come in an almost infinite range of colours, from the subtlest off-white to sandy tones, greys to taupes, the nicest neutral can be boring if it is used everywhere. The solution? Easy – darker tones for woodwork and lighter ones for walls or, if you have features such as cornices and dadoes, you can paint lighter shades above the divisions and darker ones below.

Another mistake with neutrals is to use different hues that are all the same tone – in other words, slightly different colours but the same degree of lightness or darkness. You can end up with a horrible clash. This may sound complicated, but it isn't rocket science.

To select a nice variation of tones, simply pick up a colour chart and go up or down (dark to light) within the same colour family, rather than working across from colour to colour.

A perfect finish

Finally, the plainer the colours, the more important texture becomes. So, when using neutrals, it's important to choose your finishes as carefully as you do the colours. Not only do they create visual interest, they can even affect the look of the paints themselves. A high gloss finish, for example, makes the colour appear paler, and you may need to opt for a slightly darker shade. Experiment, and enjoy – who said that neutrals were boring?

↑ This ivory wall colour is timeless and elegant.

Choosing and using neutrals

Pure white

Clean, fresh and airy, brilliant white makes rooms appear bigger and brighter, but it can also be stark and cold.

Dove

Pale greys are chic and subtle, and are beautiful with natural materials such as wicker and stone.

Stone

Mid-greys can be tough and industrial. If this look is not for you, soften with touches of lemon, pink or blue for a fashion-forward palette.

Slate

Dramatic almost-blacks make a real design statement. They are especially eye-catching when combined with splashes of bold colour.

Black

Strong and architectural, black can be used in small doses to create depth and definition in a room.

Taupe

An off-white with a definite colour but neither too yellow nor too grey, taupe makes a sophisticated background shade.

Sand

Yellowish off-whites have distinct character and add interest to a room. They will clash if used with pinkish off-whites.

Bark

Mid-browns can be warm and nurturing, reflecting the natural world – just think timber, earth and cork.

Ivory

A cool off-white, ivory looks clean and smart pretty much everywhere, and works with any other colour.

Cream

A warm off-white will cheer up a north- or east-facing room and is very easy to live with.

Magnolia

A versatile pinkish-white that was once hugely popular but is now somewhat passé. Useful for warming up a room – just don't overdo it.

Chocolate

Deep, dark and delicious, chocolate is best used in small doses (though contains no calories).

Appealing pastels and brilliant brights

Transform a room instantly by changing its colours: pale and pretty or bold and dramatic, it's time to inject instant individuality.

For some, combining colours comes naturally. For others, it helps to know a little theory first. Art books often show a colour wheel, divided into sections for the primary colours (red, blue and yellow), secondaries (purple, green and orange) and tertiaries (mixes of the above). All you need to know is that colours that are adjacent to or opposite one another on the colour wheel will co-ordinate – sometimes unexpectedly, such as fuchsia with crimson, lime green with pink, or blue with orange. And darker and lighter shades of the same colour always work well together – for example, you could put a range of blues together, from palest duck egg to rich navy.

Colour inspiration

For some less technical colour ideas, just get outside and observe naturally occurring palettes such as a floral border, a hedgerow or the feathers of a bird. Inside, look at the furnishings you already have – are there shades you can pick out to use elsewhere? What colours feel right with the architecture of your property? Remember that muted colours tend to work best in older houses – and that paint companies often have special 'historic' ranges. What colours will show off each room to its best advantage? 'Warm' colours, for example, are good in north-facing rooms, and you can usually get away with bolder or darker colours in large, light rooms. Last of all, don't forget practical considerations: painting the lower half of your hall in a dark colour, for example, might be a good idea if you have children or pets, while a very bright colour could be too distracting in a home office. Take your time and make your colour choices count. Your home will be the happier for it.

↑ The colours of this clever grouping of framed vintage fabrics echo those of the overall room scheme.

← Dark walls contrast well with white painted floors.

DISPLAYS ON WALLS
p.222

Choosing and using colours

Rose

Pretty and feminine, pale pink is perfect for a bedroom or little girl's room. Combine with pale grey or ivory for a smarter look.

Crimson

Not easy to live with as an all-over colour, bright red is great for drawing attention to focal points within a room.

Deep red

Darker reds are a cosy and warming choice for a dining room or formal sitting room. They look lovely with natural timber and stone.

Pale blue

Pale blues are calming and relaxing. Because they seem to recede, they make small or narrow rooms appear larger.

Celadon

This pale shade is on the verge between blue and green. Always appealing, its wateriness makes it ideal for a bathroom scheme.

Rich blue

The most popular colour in the world, blue is especially calming and relaxing – and is often used for bathrooms and bedrooms.

Navy

A strong colour, which is always smart and savvy, navy blue is a classic choice.

Egg yolk

What could be nicer than a warm, sunny yellow? Mellow and inviting, it also teams well with white for a crisper effect.

Orange

Used to add a dash of vibrant intensity, bright orange has a retro vibe and a definite feel-good factor.

Teal

Exotic and beautiful, teal can be warming and comforting. Team it with bright white for a standout accent shade.

Leaf

Wholesome, soothing and stress-busting – a good choice for a space in which you want to relax and unwind.

Lilac

Delicate and feminine, pale purples combine blue and red, which makes them cool and fresh as well as warm and welcoming.

Dorset Cottages
Milton Abbas 1779

The village of Milton Abbas in Dorset consists of 36 thatched cottages built in 1779. This idyllic vision of Old England is a forerunner of the model villages that were to be part of the imminent Industrial Revolution.

Surprisingly, this 18th-century village created for rural workers, was planned by two of the leading names in Georgian architecture: William Chambers, architect of Somerset House, London, and Lancelot 'Capability' Brown, the landscape gardener of Kew Gardens. This expertise cost a fortune but Lord Milton, the man who financed this model village, wasn't motivated by the interests of the community. Instead, he had decided that the original village of Milton, which had surrounded the nearby Abbey for 700 years, was spoiling the view from his brand new house and had to be demolished.

Despite his disdain for the locals, Lord Milton accepted that the old village did provide the workforce for his estate and so his plans specified that new cottages were to be built out of sight in a secluded part of the estate.

Whereas the old village had been cramped, dilapidated and regularly flooded, these new, larger houses were nestled in a valley protected by woodland. Those who were given a home there were quite lucky.

The cottages' architect, William Chambers, was better known for his grand neo-classical buildings, like the nearby Milton Estate House. With their prominent brick chimneys, thatched roofs and plain white walls, the village clearly benefited from his considerable talents. But Chambers' team of builders didn't actually work on these cottages, and the simplicity of the design was to allow novice builders to complete the work, which they did using materials reclaimed from their recently demolished homes.

The landscaping of Britain's estates was extremely popular in the mid-1700s, and perhaps the most prolific of all the landscape architects was 'Capability' Brown – so called because of his dictum that anything was 'capable of improvement'. The picturesque aspect of the village was no coincidence. Each house was laid out on a generous plot of land, allowing space between the road for a front lawn, and at the back there was a small allotment to keep a garden or – more likely – a pig.

Although Brown may well have been instrumental in the decision to demolish the old village – he was known for not letting anything get in the way of his plans – his work at Milton Abbas is considered some of his best, and the residents of the new village did eventually reap the benefits of his design.

→ Originally each house was divided into four; today some have been converted into single dwellings but others are still split as they would have been in the late Victorian period.

← Milton Abbas was one of the first fully designed settlements in England – like an 18th-century Span development.

▶ Each cottage was set on flint foundations, with outer walls using 'cob': an 18th-century mortar made from straw, chalk, rubble, and clay, bound together with cow dung. Once dry, the walls were rendered with lime and the doorways and windows hacked out, before the thatching went on top.

▶ The finished cottages were each divided into four dwellings, which meant that up to 36 people could live in just one building.

▶ The thatched roofs, which make these cottages cosy in the winter and cool in the summer, were also highly flammable; chestnut trees were planted between each house to stop fires from spreading.

▶ The main living room would have doubled as a bedroom, washroom and kitchen, with all the cooking done over an open hearth (replaced with cast iron fireplaces in the 19th century). Bread ovens were built into each hearth.

▶ The original doors would have been made from wide planks, nailed together and fitted with strap hinges, probably made by the local blacksmith.

Pattern

From the subtlest of one-colour designs to the boldest of modern retro prints, pattern adds an extra dimension to any space.

If you are in any doubt about how to add character to your home, just think pattern: a few simple pieces featuring charming, understated designs provide subtle interest. A single eye-catching, oversized pattern becomes a focal point. Or a complex combination of different patterns creates a look that is full of excitement and impact.

What pattern person are you?

▶ **Romantic:** Relaxed, timeless and feminine, these patterns focus on florals, in the form of trailing leaves and flowers or tiny, individual buds. Choose soft colours, and combine with lacy designs and sheer, floaty plains.

▶ **Modern retro:** These geometric patterns make a fabulous impact. Giant bulls eyes, chevrons and stripes are typical, or else simplified figures and animals with strong outlines. Think 1960s colour combos, such as mustard, red, orange and black.

▶ **Global traveller:** Patterns from around the globe offer an enticing world of choice. Opt for either a charmingly simple, folk style in a limited colour palette, or else a riot of intricate embroideries and colourful appliqués, plus paisleys, elaborate florals and animal motifs.

▶ **Nostalgic:** A combination of the pretty and the practical, these patterns hark back to a simpler way of life. Ticking stripes, gingham and polka dots combine with florals such as roses, hydrangea and peonies, in the colours of a country garden. A hand-printed effect is ideal.

▶ **Classic:** Scrolling patterns with arabesques and acanthus leaves, fleur-de-lys, knots and keys, garlands, medallions, laurel leaves, Tudor roses, pomegranates, urns and egg-and-dart – enduring and timeless, these patterns give a scheme a mature, considered edge.

▶ **Glamour puss:** This look is grown-up and dramatic. Include large-scale florals or figurative designs, abstracts or geometrics, on a pale background and in sophisticated colours, such as plum, aubergine, charcoal, royal blue and chocolate. Add shimmer, shine, lustre and glitter for that extra dash of luxury.

▶ **Nature lover:** The patterns of nature have eternal appeal. Flowers, leaves and trees, simply representational or subtly abstract, are easy on the eye and straightforward to combine with most decorative schemes. Greens, greys and browns, punctuated by floral shades, predominate in this pattern choice.

Types of pattern

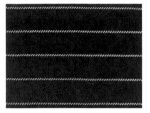

Pinstripe

Slim, parallel stripes, often on a dark background. Typical of men's suiting but looks smart in an interior.

Ticking

A medium stripe on a white background often used for mattress covers. A nostalgic and simple look.

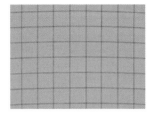

Windowpane

Slim, single-colour stripes criss-cross to form a pattern of very large checks.

Polka dot

A playful pattern of small spots, placed closely together on a plain background.

Tartan

Alternating bands of colour create a distinctive check usually associated with Scottish kilts.

Gingham

Small checks made by coloured horizontal and vertical stripes of the same width on a white background.

Hound's tooth

Small check design with a jagged shape. Traditionally twill, woven in black and white.

Herringbone

This weave is made of small zigzags. In a larger form it is similar to a chevron pattern.

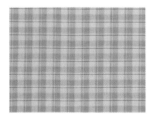

Madras

Originating in India, this informal pattern features colourful stripes that cross to form uneven checks.

Toile de Jouy

Originally from France, these patterns show pastoral scenes, often in dark red, blue or black, on a pale background.

Paisley

Of Persian or Indian origin, these patterns feature the distinctive boteh, a teardrop-shaped motif.

Ikat

Tie-dyed yarns are woven into distinctive patterns that are often based around zigzags or diamond shapes.

Using pattern

It's not as hard as you may think to make patterns look great in your space. Our guidelines will help you to take the plunge.

Are you worried about venturing away from the safety of plains? Well, set your concerns aside, because it really is easy when you know how. You can introduce pattern in all sorts of ways, from the print on a vase to a whole feature wall, a small cushion to an eye-catching rug, a lampshade to a fabulous curtain. Don't be nervous: follow a few straightforward pattern guidelines and simply take it step by step.

1 Narrow down your pattern choices by working out which styles you like best. Check out wallpaper and fabric pattern books in decorating stores, look through magazines and books, and don't be afraid to borrow ideas from other sources, such as friends' homes, restaurants, shops, galleries and hotels.

2 Would you prefer just a dash of pattern to enliven an otherwise plain room, or a striking combination of patterns for an all-over look? If you are feeling tentative, start slowly, and built it up in layers as your confidence increases.

3 In bigger rooms, large-scale patterns have amazing impact, while smaller rooms are better suited to medium- or small-scale patterns – unless you want to make a particular feature out of a tiny room by adding a dramatically huge pattern, of course.

4 Make a mood board (see opposite) to ensure that your patterns work perfectly together. Try to obtain the largest possible samples of fabric and wallpaper and, before you make any final decisions, hang them in place to get a really good idea of their effect.

5 Match the key colours of your patterns exactly and the overall look will co-ordinate effortlessly.

6 Bear in mind that loose, open patterns give a visual 'breather', while intricate patterns with closely placed designs have more drama. A variety of densities give balance and interest. The same goes for scale, too.

7 Don't forget that very small patterns are only really noticeable close up; from a distance they look like a plain colour.

8 Not sure what patterns go with what? Limit your combinations to designs that originate from the same era or stylistic aesthetic.

9 Stripes are the workhorses of the pattern world. Match the colours and they will co-ordinate brilliantly with more intricate patterns.

10 Keep experimenting. Try putting a few patterns together and, if they don't look quite right, change them round until you achieve the look you want.

How to make a mood board

Creating a mood board will help to ensure that all the elements you have chosen for a room makeover will look good together.

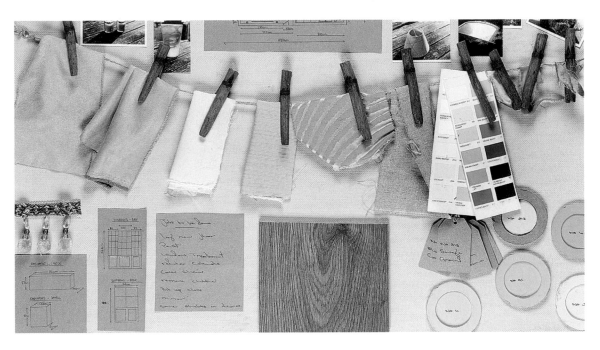

It's the professional way to visualise your design before spending money and, possibly, making expensive mistakes. Start by collecting swatches of fabric, wallpaper, flooring and paints, and photographs or sketches of furniture, light fittings and other elements of your room scheme. Try to keep the samples roughly in proportion to the size they would be in real life. Now take a large piece of white card, and simply place the samples on, roughly in accordance with where they will be in the room – flooring at the bottom, lights near the top and furnishings in the middle.

When the board is finished, stand back and assess the overall effect. Do any elements jar? Should you make more of one feature and less of another? Move your swatches, pictures and sketches around, take some away and add others until you are completely happy with the overall effect.

↑ Interior designers use mood boards to explain design ideas to their clients.

Texture

How does your space feel? It's textures that turn a space from frumpy to fabulous and really bring a room to life.

A varied and interesting use of texture underpins every design scheme. To an extent, we do it without thinking – putting a knitted throw over the arm of a leather sofa, or placing a wicker basket beside a stone fire surround, for example – but it is still worth taking a moment or two to ensure that your room contains a pleasing variety of interesting textures. Because not only is the right surface in the right area a functional necessity, but textures enable us to relate to our surroundings in a way that is instinctive, comforting and down to earth.

Talking texture

In most rooms, the backbone textures are smooth and understated – perhaps wooden floorboards, linen upholstery and papered walls – and the interest lies in how these are combined with other elements. To make a bedroom cosier, for example, you could add a fluffy rug, velvet curtains and quilted eiderdowns. Or, to emphasise a bright and airy living room, finishing touches might include sheer curtains, feather-trimmed cushions and glass or chrome lamp bases. If you use understated colour schemes and simple patterns, your textures will speak for themselves: sisal, shell, stone, driftwood or wicker – all beautiful, subtle and natural textures with masses of character.

Texture has an important part to play in the overall style of a room, too. Modern rooms tend to feature harder, shinier surfaces (stainless steel, chrome and mirror), whereas a vintage or ethnic look (with quilts, knitting, embroidery and lace) is more rustic and varied in texture.

↓ A textural rug and cushions add another dimension to this understated decorative scheme.

Varieties of texture

Linen

The slightly nubby, lustrous surface of woven linen gives it a lovely, subtle interest.

Leather

Natural yet hardwearing, leather has subtle creases and wrinkles that add personality.

Riven slate

Tough, long-lasting and durable, slate comes in a variety of surfaces – the riven texture has a craggy, cracked appeal.

Glazed ceramic

Ultra-smooth and ultra-shiny, glazed ceramic reflects light and contrasts well with soft fabrics.

Cashmere

Super-soft and luxurious, this expensive fibre is the ultimate in cosiness.

Coir matting

Nubby, hairy, rough and tough, coir is just one of many natural floorings that come in a variety of weaves and finishes.

Wool felt

Thick and soft, felted wool is natural, even rustic, and offers a feeling of warmth and nostalgia.

Flokati

Flokati rugs have a deep-pile, hairy surface that feels cosy underfoot.

Velvet

Velvet is soft, warm and luxurious to the touch, thanks to its short raised pile. Combines nicely with smoother surfaces.

Silk satin

A really smooth and shiny, lustrous surface. Contrast with rougher textures – such as a satin trim on a woollen blanket.

Chrome

Super shiny, hard and reflective, chromed metal works well as a highlight in a modern scheme.

Fake fur

Fur has immediate appeal when you want a surface that is incredibly soft and comforting.

Regency Square
Brighton 1818–28

The town of Brighton, on the south coast of England, first became a popular destination for holidaymakers at the end of the 19th century when George, Prince of Wales, commissioned John Nash to build the flamboyant Royal Pavilion. When the Napoleonic Wars ended in 1815, Brighton became a fashionable playground for the rich and famous and a housing boom followed. Most buildings in Brighton, however, reflected a neo-classical taste that was more mainstream than the Royal Pavilion.

This Regency Square, constructed from 1818, was one of the first of its kind built in Brighton. It was the brainchild of developer Joshua Hanson, who realised that rental boltholes by the sea were in high demand, and employed architect William Mackie to appeal to this market. Mackie kept proportions modest and built a central communal garden to appeal to out-of-town tenants. But the true genius of building around a square meant that all houses had a sea view – something still sought after today.

Mackie moved on to different projects, leaving the builders to finish his design. However, a combination of corner-cutting and the whims of investors meant that the completed square is far from uniform: the buildings vary in height and some have curved fronts while others are flat, some share verandas while others have none.

These houses are as fashionable today as they would have been when they were first built. And even though they only gained Grade II listed status in the 1970s, the original landowner had the forethought to put in place some rules to protect the look of the square. A covenant stated that stucco plaster – a mixture made with sand and lime – had to be kept below the balcony, while the honey-coloured local brick was to remain on show above. In fact, the brick is thought to be so local that it could have been dug up from beneath the square itself.

▶ The main sitting room would have been upstairs in order to make the most of the sea views.

▶ The raised ground floor was originally used as a dining room and a parlour – a reception room where visitors were received.

▶ Balconies were originally decorative rather than functional, often featuring ornate ironwork. You would have to climb through the window to sit out on them.

▶ The proportions of the rooms tend to get smaller and smaller the higher you go in the house. This is due to the Regency fashion for cramming in as many rooms as possible – and while lower floors were for entertaining and relaxing, the top floors were where the servants and children slept.

▶ Kitchens were originally situated in the basement or at the back of the house, to minimise the risk of fire.

↗ The variety of styles in the finished houses is clear. Mackie's square was used as a prototype for later designs that became grander and more uniform.

→ The square features in a diorama of the seafront by A. H. Wilds, 1833.

PERIOD CHARACTER p.9

CASE STUDY | A Light, Bright Space

This living/dining room needed to serve a variety of functions, so it was important to zone the space thoughtfully and achieve a blend of practicality and style.

BRIEF

Eric and Marta were living in this rented flat with their two young daughters and this room, which they saw as a living/dining room, had not been decorated since they moved in. They wanted a fresh, contemporary style in light, calm colours, and to make better use of the space. Storage was important, both for the children's toys and for Eric's records and DJ equipment. As the property is rented there were limits on what could be done: the carpet and chandeliers could not be changed, and pictures had to hang from the picture rails and not be attached to the walls themselves. Eric and Marta wanted to keep their comfortable family sofa and had some other pieces that could be upcycled.

BEFORE

Bright pattern

Splashes of colour

↑ The designer's mood board is a great mix of photographs, artwork, paint swatches and actual pieces, but lacks a floor plan.

→ An upcycled cupboard provides children's storage next to a chalkboard wall.

▶ The walls are now clean and white both above and below the picture rail, which really maximises the feeling of space.

▶ The wall lights were modernised by turning them upside down and adding new, spray-painted shades.

▶ The shelves and recess cupboard have also been painted white to avoid breaking up the walls either side of the fireplace. One gives a home to Eric's DJ equipment, while a metal storage cabinet underneath houses his records.

▶ The children's play area has been defined by a colourful rug, and a clever blackboard breaks up the white wall and provides a place for the girls to draw.

AFTER

↖ Rugs help to define the room into different zones for dining, playing, relaxing and working.

← In Eric's DJ area, framed album covers provide colour and interest against the white wall.

CASE STUDY | Regency Glamour

This large room underwent a radical change from a glorified storage area to a cool, sophisticated living and dining space.

BRIEF

Julie had bought her house 18 months earlier; it was one of only a few properties in the square not to have been converted into flats because it was previously used as a hotel. The room awaiting renovation was a double aspect living and dining room with typically high ceilings and beautiful original plaster coving and cornicing. It was being used as a storage area while the family was renovating the rest of the house. Julie wanted the room to feel welcoming and homely, but sophisticated too: a place where they could socialise as a family and entertain friends. Her vision was a grown-up and glamorous 'Hollywood Regency' style room.

BEFORE

→ The designer's proposal includes paint and fabric swatches that are true both to the brief and to the Regency origins of the room. The map and period photograph also provided inspiration.

Regency period paint swatches

A striking wall display

Map and period photograph

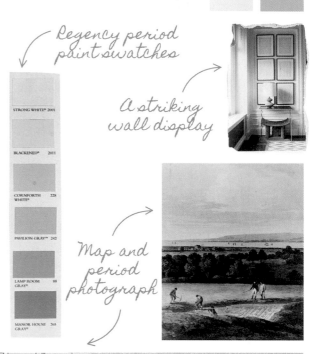

STRONG WHITE® 2001

BLACKENED® 2011

CORNFORTH WHITE® 228

PAVILION GRAY™ 242

LAMP ROOM GRAY® 88

MANOR HOUSE GRAY® 265

Bonnet

Wesquage Pond

Bonnet Shores Beach

Boston Neck

Watson Pier

JUDGE'S VIEW
'The mural is very strong
and the panelling is
really successful. A punch
of colour would have
highlighted the room
a bit more.'

▶ Walls painted in two tones of warm grey are subtle and easy to live with.

▶ The large room now has clearly defined spaces for dining and relaxing, unified by the colour scheme.

▶ The new wool carpet is luxurious, as are the carefully chosen accessories, such as the starburst mirror and touches of gilt.

▶ The designer has re-used much of Julie's furniture, painting some pieces to match the walls.

← Painted pine beading recreates the look of traditional panelling.

↓ The room is now flooded with light and is certainly a grown-up and glamorous space.

AFTER

← Accent cushions with an eye-catching print are a great finishing touch.

DESIGN HIGHLIGHT
↗ The bold mural was a brave choice and helps to make the room feel furnished and reinforces the Regency style; it was one of Julie's favourite features.

IDEAS FOR FEATURE WALLS p.91

← Julie's French armoire has been painted in the same two greys as the walls so that it blends in. Having been decluttered, it now contains an attractive display of glassware.

→ The same wall colours have been used in both halves of the room in order to give a sense of continuity.

CASE STUDY | Rustic Elegance

The last room left to be decorated in a large house, this kitchen-diner was full of wonderful furniture but needed a coherent decorative scheme to pull everything together.

BRIEF

Like Julie, Trix also lived in one of the few whole houses still left in the square. She had redecorated the entire property, but had run out of ideas for this raised ground floor kitchen-diner. She wanted new worktops for her freestanding oak kitchen, which was in need of a clean but otherwise was in good condition. The floor was also oak and she wanted it extended into the dining area, which was carpeted. Her large cherry wood dining table provided a centrepiece for the dining area, and she had already started reupholstering the chairs. She favoured a blue colour scheme complemented by neutral tones.

Sketches and a floor plan

↓ The designer's mood board is extremely comprehensive, featuring paint samples, fabric swatches and trimmings, photographic ideas and a detailed floor plan.

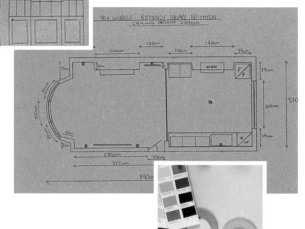

BEFORE

Fabric and trimmings

JUDGE'S VIEW

'It feels so much bigger. One floor unifying the space transforms it. I don't mind the curtains and walls being exactly the same colour, but the turquoise splash of colour is a bit too subtle.'

▶ A pale, neutral wall colour helps the room feel larger and less cluttered.

▶ A range of paint effects used on the kitchen cabinets adds to the rustic, French-style look.

▶ The new wooden floor was a big expense, but gives continuity between the two spaces.

▶ Moving a small storage unit away from the window allows in more light, and turning it into an island has made the whole space more efficient and easy to use.

▶ Extra storage above the oven and fridge frees up clutter from the worktops and cupboards.

↓ The blue that Trix loves, but that previously made the room feel dark, was used for finishing touches around the room.

→ Shelving and useful hooks provide additional storage.

AFTER

DESIGN HIGHLIGHT

↓ This wall unit combines practical storage with an attractive display of kitchen kit. Open shelves and hanging space, rather than cupboards with doors, has an informal, rustic look.

↗ A painted mirror on the mantelpiece.

↓ Trix's classic furniture looks perfectly at home in the elegant room.

↓ The useful new island was made by sawing the top off a unit and cleverly repositioning it.

Project

The designers at Regency Square were each given a simple plaster bust to upcycle. Painting plaster is straightforward – and you can embellish your design however you wish.

A fun headphone holder.

A distressed paint effect.

Gold spray paint for some Hollywood bling.

HOW TO PAINT A PLASTER STATUE

1 Seal your plaster statue with a sealant such as polyurethane. If your statue is likely to be exposed to outdoor elements or humidity, it is best to use weatherproof polyurethane. Apply three coats of sealant and allow to dry completely between each application.

2 If the surface is uneven or bubbly sand down with a fine grain sandpaper, and then apply one more thin coat of polyurethane, using a paint brush. This will make the top layer as smooth as possible for painting.

3 Apply a base colour over the entire surface of the statue, using a paint brush and acrylic paint. Allow the paint to dry, and then start to add other colours according to your design. When dry apply one more coat of sealant, making sure there are no bubbles in the polyurethane.

Planning makes perfect

If you want a home that functions perfectly and looks gorgeous, careful planning is the key.

Good planning means considering every aspect of your interior design, from who will do the work, to what materials, furnishings and finishing touches you need to buy. It means drawing up a budget, understanding rules and regulations and getting to grips with safety. It may mean employing a professional, or learning a new skill. And it means the most exciting thing of all – that you are getting started!

First things first
Although you may be tempted to rush in and try to change everything at once, now is the time to stand back and take some sensible decisions. Is the property structurally safe and sound? Is it warm

enough in winter? Have you got plenty of hot water whenever you need it? Do your windows stick when you try to open them; are your stairs creaky or is your plaster crumbling away? Before you do anything decorative, it is much more important to focus on repairs and renovations. Buy a new boiler before the three-piece suite (better to be cosy on an old sofa than freezing on a new one) and mend your gutters before you repaint. In the long run, you will be happy that you got your priorities right.

↑ Make good the structure of your property before starting any decorating project.

Repairs and renovations

Before you embark on a decorating project make sure your home is as sound as it can be. Here are a few common problems to watch out for.

Cracks in walls

Cracks are often caused by tiny movements of your house and may be nothing to worry about. However, you should get professional advice from a qualified chartered surveyor if a crack is more than 5mm (¼in) wide, if it keeps getting bigger, if you have more than one crack in a room, or if a crack appears outside as well as inside.

Creaking stairs

Creaks are caused by timbers moving and rubbing against each other. First, identify which tread is causing the problem. If you can get at the staircase from below, it should be quite easy to glue and screw the wedges that hold the tread in place. If not, then try screwing up through the riser at an angle so as to secure it to the tread above. Or use steel corner braces. Squirting wood glue into gaps may also help.

Sticking or rattling sash windows

Old sash windows need regular attention: if you are confident in your skills, you could dismantle, ease, adjust, re-cord and reassemble them; if not, there are a number of specialist companies who can do it for you. Draught-proof them at the same time (see below).

Damp patches

These are often caused by blocked, cracked or disconnected gutters, downpipes or drains. Sort these out first. Check for leaking plumbing, and cracks in external walls, too. Rising damp is often caused by the ground level outside being too high. Reduce it in order to let the wall breathe. If you have mould on cold surfaces, especially in bathrooms or cupboards, the damp is caused by condensation. Improve heating and ventilation, and it should be resolved.

Draughts

Try draught-proofing strips around windows and doors – the best option is a specialist seal fitted into a cut-in rebate (compression seals for hinged windows; wipers for sliding sashes). Shutters or heavy, floor-to-ceiling curtains are also effective. For windows that you seldom open, secondary glazing is ideal. Cover keyholes, letter slots and cat flaps on external doors, and add an old-fashioned 'sausage dog' along the bottom edge. Seal gaps at the base of the skirting boards with foam strips, silicon mastic or thin slivers of matching timber. To fill gaps between old floorboards, use fillets of balsa wood or lengths of string, which can be stained, glued and pushed into place.

Leaking roof

Stand away from the house and use binoculars to check the roof tiles, chimney stack, rainwater goods, mortar and flashing (lead or zinc sheet that covers joins between roof and walls or chimney). Then go into the loft and check that timbers are dry and solid and there are no damp patches on the ceiling. You may be able to safely clear gutters and repair downpipes, but most rooftop jobs should be left to a professional.

Blocked chimneys

Poorly maintained fireplaces and flues are the biggest causes of fires in old buildings. Have your chimney swept regularly, and use a smoke pellet to check it for air tightness. If your flue is faulty and cannot be mended from outside, or if you are fitting a stove, you will need to install a flue liner first.

Getting the builders in

Whether you are converting a loft or fitting a new cupboard, a skilled and reliable tradesperson is worth his or her weight in gold.

When you hire a builder you must establish a professional and good-natured working relationship, in which everyone knows who is responsible for what, and exactly how each task will be carried out. Good builders are able to advise and help solve problems – but remember, it is your money and your home, so the final decisions must be yours. Ensure that your plans are fully developed, down to the last detail, before work starts.

Order of work

In all but the smallest of projects, there is an established order of work that it is advisable to follow, especially if the project involves two or more different trades. Sometimes a plumber, an electrician and a plasterer (for example) can all work on site at the same time; but often you will find that one element of your project can't be started until another has finished. A well thought-through schedule is crucial, and good project management – either from a professional or yourself – will help keep things moving. There will be inevitable delays and frustrations, perhaps as you discover unexpected problems with the property, materials arrive late or a workman doesn't turn up. It's how you handle these problems that counts.

Once you have got your finances together, developed your designs, received planning and other necessary permissions and agreed terms with the builder, the first thing to do is empty out the space, protect surfaces and erect any scaffolding. Although every project is different, in general, the 'first fix' stage involves demolition and clearing, and the main construction – foundations, floors, walls and ceilings. It also includes initial carpentry, such as door frames and windows, and getting cables and pipes in place for electricity and plumbing. The 'second fix' covers everything else needed to complete the project, including plastering, installing radiators, baths, WCs and sinks, connecting appliances, wiring switches, sockets and light fittings, hanging doors, applying skirtings, architraves and other features, fitting kitchens, tiling, decorating and flooring. Last of all comes the 'snagging', when you or your project manager details anything that's not quite right so as to ensure you get the perfect finish.

Workmen on site

When you are employing a tradesperson, it is important to get the details sorted out in advance. Try to establish the following to avoid clashes with neighbours or yourself before the job gets started:

► The order of work.

► What hours they will arrive and leave.

► How they will get in and who locks up (if you're not living there).

► Where they can park and store equipment.

► Who will clear out the working areas in advance.

► Who will clear the mess up afterwards.

► What loo they can use.

► Where they can clean their tools.

► Whether or not they can play a radio.

► Whether they can bring pets to the property.

Finding a good builder

It's the eternally worrying question: how to find a good builder (or plumber, or electrician, or tiler – or even an architect, or interior designer). Before you take anyone on, check that they are properly qualified and have adequate insurance for the job. You could also ask for references from previous clients.

▶ **Personal recommendation:** If friends, family or neighbours have had work done recently and were happy with it, grab the details without hesitation.

▶ **Professional and trade associations:** Look up the relevant association and you can often simply type in your postcode to be given a list of local members. Some associations offer guarantee schemes.

▶ **The internet:** A variety of sites offer to find you a good local builder, often by recommendation. Check out their credentials first, though.

▶ **Local paper:** Small ads can be a great source of local tradespeople but, as with the internet, you'll need to check them out before hiring them.

▶ **Local building works:** See a skip outside a nearby house? Pluck up your courage and politely ask the house owner whether they would recommend their builder. They will probably be only too happy to share their experiences with you.

The specialists: who does what?

▶ **Architects** design buildings, extensions and renovations, and produce specifications and technical drawings for the contractors. They advise on whether the plans for your property will require planning permission and/or need to comply with building regulations.

▶ **Quantity surveyors** manage the costs on larger projects.

▶ **Structural engineers** work with architects to ensure that new structures or alterations are safe.

▶ **Project managers** are responsible for the planning, design, execution, monitoring and closure of a project.

▶ **Main contractors** provide the material, labour and equipment to carry out a project.

▶ **Sub-contractors** include plumbers, electricians, tilers or glaziers, and are often employed by main contractors for specialist tasks.

▶ **Interior designers** plan spaces for function, comfort and good looks.

Going green

If you are doing work on your home, now is the time to see whether you can add any environmentally friendly features that will save you money (and the planet) in the long run. Some eco measures, such as installing ground source heat pumps and wind turbines, are really only suitable for new builds or major renovations, but solar panels and rainwater recycling are more feasible for many people. And there are plenty of less expensive options, too, including fitting double or secondary glazing, installing water-saving shower heads and insulating your loft, or even such simple ideas as connecting an energy monitor or switching to energy-saving light bulbs.

Doing it yourself

Doing it yourself is fun and economical, until something goes wrong, that is. If you have the skills, the time and the right tools or equipment, DIY is great. If not, you'll need to bite the bullet and GSI (get someone in).

How to learn DIY

▶ **DIY parent:** A patient parent who knows what he or she is doing – and will even lend you the right tool if you haven't got it – is ideal. If you haven't got a DIY parent, perhaps you have a handy friend or neighbour who would be prepared to show you the basics.

▶ **Classes:** Adult education classes are a great place in which to learn all sorts of DIY skills, from introductory courses to professional qualifications, from an experienced teacher with all necessary tools at hand.

▶ **The Internet:** DIY videos posted on the internet can be really helpful. Just make sure you choose one that comes from a reliable source.

▶ **Books, magazines and leaflets:** They are no substitute for the personal touch, but you can still glean plenty of basic information, as well as tips and tricks, from written sources. Specific in-store advice leaflets can often be particularly good.

→ Creating bespoke shelving such as this is not as hard as you may think. There are many ways to learn DIY skills.

DIY or GSI?

▶ How handy are you (be honest). If you don't have the aptitude, don't be tempted to try anything too tricky.

▶ Is your toolbox up to the job? Basic kit is fine for many projects, but more complex tasks may require other tools, which you will need to buy or hire.

▶ Do you live in an older property? Uneven walls and floors make even straightforward DIY more challenging.

▶ Have you got the time? It is easy to underestimate how long it will take to complete a job, especially if you have never done it before.

▶ Does the project involve heavy lifting? Don't be a hero - get someone to help.

▶ Does it involve gas or electricity? Then don't hesitate to call in a professional.

Toolbox basics

Tape measure

A 5m length is useful. Buy one that is easy to read, lockable and that retracts easily.

Claw hammer

Both for driving in nails and levering them out. Available in different sizes and weights – 16oz is a good general choice.

Pliers

Look for comfortable grips that are insulated against electric shocks. Standard pliers for general use; fine nose for fiddly jobs.

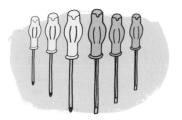

Set of screwdrivers

Cross-headed and flat-headed, in a range of sizes, for different uses around the home.

Set of Allen keys

It's amazing how many items need one of these little keys to tighten or loosen them.

Hacksaw

For small jobs, a junior hacksaw is fine, and will cut plastic, metal and small pieces of wood. Buy a set of spare blades, too.

Trimming knife

These have replaceable, retractable blades. A standard blade will cut thinner materials; special blades cut wood, laminates and metal.

Spirit level

This is essential to make sure your work is straight. A 600mm level is a good length.

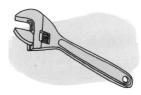

Adjustable spanner

Use it with a variety of nuts and bolts; 10in is a good size.

Paint brushes

At least five sizes is useful (1, 1½, 2, 2½ and 3in). Choose natural bristles for oil-based paints, or synthetic for use with water-based paints.

Paint roller and tray

Short-pile rollers are ideal for flat surfaces; medium for slightly uneven surfaces; long for exterior or textured surfaces.

Torch

Essential when working in dark corners, or when your power has gone off.

Safety

Never take shortcuts where safety is concerned. Some DIY jobs can be hazardous, especially if you haven't had a great deal of experience or training. Use your common sense and avoid accidents.

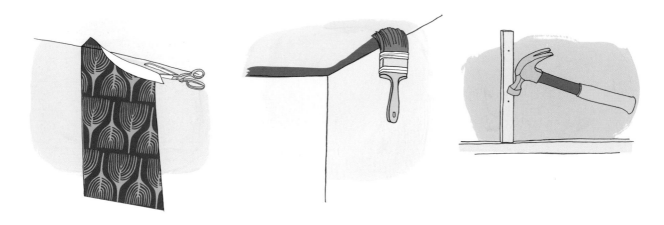

▶ Always use the right tool for the job. Don't be tempted to bodge – not only could it be risky, but the work is unlikely to turn out well.

▶ If you have hired a tool you're not familiar with, read the operating instructions carefully and, if in doubt, ask for a run-through before you leave the hire shop.

▶ Use cordless power tools when possible. When using one with a cord, check that the cord is in good condition, and use a circuit breaker.

▶ Lift heavy weights with care: keep your back straight and bend from the knee. Get help if necessary.

▶ Ladders are a major cause of accidents. Place on firm, even ground and ask someone to hold the bottom. The golden rule is to keep three limbs in contact with the ladder at all times. Never over-reach. Get help when using an extension ladder.

▶ Never use tools that are blunt or broken.

▶ Wear appropriate clothing – sensible shoes with good grips, shirts that don't flap about, goggles, a dust mask and ear defenders when necessary. Tie long hair out of the way and take off jewellery.

▶ When painting, using toxic materials or creating lots of dust, keep the room well ventilated.

▶ Don't smoke while doing DIY, and keep children and pets away from your working area.

▶ Plan your work in advance. Don't rush or cut corners.

▶ Clear up as soon as possible once you have finished, and store tools and equipment safely.

▶ Keep a first-aid kit and a fire extinguisher handy, just in case.

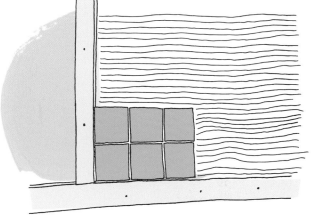

↓→ Sanding floors and tiling walls are two home improvement jobs you can do yourself.

Home improvement jobs to tackle yourself

- ▶ Painting
- ▶ Tiling and grouting
- ▶ Making curtains, blinds and cushion covers
- ▶ Wallpapering
- ▶ Putting up a shelf
- ▶ Sanding floorboards
- ▶ Filling holes and cracks in walls
- ▶ Repairing patches of rotten woodwork
- ▶ Laying laminate flooring
- ▶ Bleeding radiators
- ▶ Insulating the loft

Rules and regulations

Small changes to the design of your interior are unlikely to concern your local planning department, but if you are considering bigger alterations, such as an extension or loft conversion, you may need to get planning permission. And if your building is listed or if you live in a conservation area, be extra careful to check what you can and can't do.

Building regulations cover practically every aspect of building work to your home, from the energy efficiency of new windows to electrical installations, and it is important that you comply with them. You can usually leave this aspect of the work to the professional you employ, but if you are doing it yourself, check with the building control department of your local authority.

Staying on budget

Whether your project is large or small, it is vital to keep in careful control of your costs.

Start by deciding who is going to do the work. If it is possible to do it yourself, you will save money – provided you can do it properly. If you need to employ a builder or other tradesperson for anything other than the smallest of jobs, draw up a specification in advance, covering both the labour and the materials required, meet the people on site, and get at least three quotes (not estimates). Remember that the cheapest quote is not always the best.

The dos and don'ts of budgeting

▶ **DO** try to think of everything. It's worth making the effort at the beginning to plan every last detail. In the long run, it will save you time, money and stress.

▶ **DON'T** change your mind or add extra work halfway through your project. It will irritate your builder and end up costing you more.

▶ **DO** be realistic with your budget. If you are overly optimistic about costs, you are bound to get caught out.

▶ **DO** allow at least a 10 per cent contingency. Unfortunately, unexpected problems are a fact of life.

▶ **DO** plan to get jobs such as brickwork, tiling and plastering all done at the same time. It should save time, money and mess.

▶ **DON'T** forget to add in the costs of obtaining planning permission and alternative accommodation, if you have to move out while the work is going on.

▶ **DON'T** pay your builder up front. Reputable builders have accounts with trade suppliers so there should be no need. Agree a method of payment (usually in instalments) in writing, and stick to it.

▶ **DO** keep back 10 per cent at the end of the work to cover possible defects. When everything is complete, make a list of 'snags' and ask your builder to remedy them. Pay the final amount promptly once you are satisfied.

Three ways to reduce your costs

1 Do at least some of the work yourself (or get a DIY-savvy friend to help).

2 Economise on materials (can you buy second-hand, wait for a sale or get to an outlet store?).

3 Carry out the work in stages.

↑ Buying furniture at charity shops or on online auction sites can help reduce costs.

A sample kitchen budget

Building work: preparing floors, walls and ceilings .... £XX
Plumbing .... £XX
Electrics .... £XX
Installation of kitchen .... £XX
Fitting flooring .... £XX
Tiling .... £XX
Decorating .... £XX
Fitted and/or unfitted storage: cupboards, shelves, racks etc .... £XX
Worktops and splashbacks .... £XX
Flooring .... £XX
Wallcoverings .... £XX
Lighting .... £XX
Heating .... £XX
Window treatments .... £XX
Sink, waste and taps .... £XX
Cooker, hob, extractor .... £XX
Microwave .... £XX
Fridge/freezer .... £XX
Dishwasher .... £XX
Washing machine, tumble dryer .... £XX
Small appliances .... £XX
Waste bin .... £XX
Dining table/breakfast bar.................. £XX
Chairs/stools .... £XX
Table linen .... £XX
Crockery, glassware, cutlery .... £XX
Pots, pans, knives, chopping board, scales and other equipment .... £XX
TOTAL .... **£XX**

A sample bathroom budget

Building work: preparing floors, walls and ceilings .... £XX
Plumbing .... £XX
Electrics .... £XX
Carpentry .... £XX
Installation of fixtures, fittings and flooring ... £XX
Plastering .... £XX
Tiling .... £XX
Painting and decorating .... £XX
Bath .... £XX
Bath side/end panels .... £XX
Bath taps .... £XX
Bath waste/plug .... £XX
Shower mixer .... £XX
Shower tray .... £XX
Showerhead .... £XX
Shower enclosure .... £XX
Shower waste .... £XX
Basin .... £XX
Basin taps .... £XX
Basin waste/plug .... £XX
Basin support brackets or pedestal .... £XX
Vanity unit/cupboard .... £XX
WC .... £XX
WC seat .... £XX
Toilet roll holder .... £XX
Radiator .... £XX
Extractor fan .... £XX
Underfloor heating .... £XX
Flooring .... £XX
Paint .... £XX
Lighting .... £XX
Countertops .... £XX
Mirror .... £XX
Accessories (stool, linen basket, towels, soap dish, loo brush) .... £XX
TOTAL .... **£XX**

Georgian Townhouses
Liverpool 1827

By the 19th century, Liverpool had become a hub of international trade based on imported commodities such as tobacco, salt and cotton, which supplied the textile mills of Manchester and Lancashire. The port also dealt in a darker, more profitable trade – slavery. Abolished in 1807, the slave trade was instrumental in raising Liverpool from a struggling port to one of the most prosperous trading centres in the world.

Local businessmen, who had made their fortunes as merchants, shipbrokers and industrialists, looked to property development as a new venture and, working with local regulations, they created new streets, which were built for profit as much as town planning. Small plots were bought and built on by different companies, sparking a trend for spec-built housing that would dominate British building for the next 150 years. The houses were built to last just a few decades, but thanks to the rugged and well-engineered design, their simple and magnificent architecture is still in evidence today.

This imposing Georgian terrace, on the industrial outskirts of Liverpool, was built in 1827. These houses reflect the predominant architectural styles of the Georgian period and avoid the new flourishes of the upcoming Regency style. This type of Georgian architecture was highly influenced by the neo-Greek style. The developers of these houses copied the townhouse design that was popular throughout the country and fused it with some minimal neo-classical motifs, such as the Doric columns that frame the front doors.

Edward Falkner, who bought and developed the terrace and its neighbouring square, was something of a local legend. At the age of 28 he was appointed High Sherriff of Liverpool. Ten years later, reacting to the threat of an imminent French attack, it is said that he rallied 1,000 men in just one hour to defend the port. Hearing of this, the French were scared off, and Faulkner became a national hero.

▶ Windows in Georgian houses were almost all sashes, with standardised panes of glass divided by thin, delicate wooden glazing bars. On the ground or lower ground floor windows were kept short in order to help stabilise the structure; first floor windows were tall and elegantly expansive; second floor windows were shorter; third floor windows were roughly square.

▶ The most important rooms were on the first floor – the main dining and drawing room – while the reception room was usually on the ground floor.

▶ The kitchen, scullery and servants' quarters would all have been located below stairs. The larder and pantry were sandwiched together with the basement kitchen between.

▶ Georgian colours began by being quite heavy and dark, but by this period were becoming lighter, with more pastel shades, stones, greys, pea greens, Wedgwood blue and dusky pinks on the walls, and stronger colours for dining rooms and decorative details.

▶ Georgians would have used heavy wallpapers and ornate furniture to impress their guests; until the 1800s wallpaper was actually made from rags.

▶ Segmented shutters meant you could control the amount of light coming into a room.

→ These elegant Georgian townhouses were built for Liverpool's merchants and businessmen.

CASE STUDY

The Old & the New

Busy families often don't have time for home improvements, and this large Georgian home was in need of a design scheme that showed it off to its best advantage.

BRIEF

Although Gaynor, Andrew and their two children had lived in their house for nearly four years, they wanted it to feel more homely and have some life breathed into its stark interior. Gaynor felt the house was too bland, and that it would benefit from a smart, country-style transformation. The family were keen for more storage in their hallway to conceal a lot of typical family 'junk' and, as the original features had previously been removed, they were hoping for some of them to be brought back. As well as the hallway, the rooms to be made over included the living room, their daughter's bedroom and a guest bedroom.

BEFORE

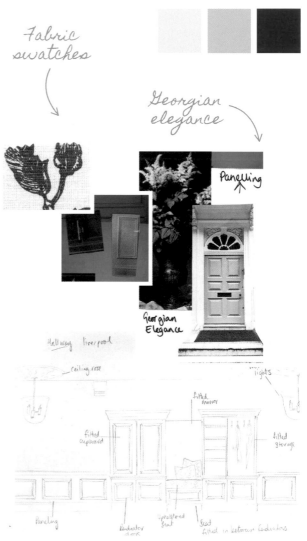

Fabric swatches

Georgian elegance

Panelling

Georgian Elegance

↑ The designer's proposal includes detailed plans to show the homeowners exactly what they could expect.

↓ The built-in cupboards blend in well with the scheme and provide much-needed storage for the family.

AFTER

▶ The family's storage needs have been met by adding cupboards over the radiators; one has been left open, with hooks to store coats.

▶ The greyish-green colour scheme is elegant and timeless.

▶ To recreate a Georgian feel, panelling has been made using beading and a dado rail added.

▶ For the seat cushions and door curtain, floral fabrics inject a dash of pattern and texture.

▶ The glass lampshades are full of period character.

↑ More colour and life has been added to the scheme with a large plant in a Georgian-style urn.

A NEAT AND TIDY HALL p.126

CASE STUDY | Living in Harmony

This living space and music room needed to fulfil a number of different functions while remaining warm and comfortable.

BRIEF

The living room was mainly used by the family's lodgers, and also by Gaynor and the children for playing the piano and music lessons – so the piano had to be incorporated into the design. Andrew also used the room for his work, so it needed to serve all these functions while staying in keeping with the rest of the house. Gaynor and Andrew felt their style was traditional with modern touches, but not too over the top. Gaynor preferred textured and geometric patterned fabrics, such as tweeds and tartans, rather than florals, and favoured a palette that included cornflower blue and pale sage green. They wanted a room that was warm and bright rather than cold and moody.

BEFORE

Colour inspiration

→ The designer has created a feature fireplace that matches the colour scheme within the room.

Feature fireplace

→ The large back wall has been decorated with a richly coloured mural.

▶ The large mural is both colourful and dramatic, but it has been placed to the side of the sofa so the homeowners will not have to look at it when they are relaxing.

▶ As with the hall, wood panelling and a dado rail have been added to give the room a Georgian feel.

▶ A fireplace has been reintroduced to give the room a focal point; hand-painted tiles add colour and interest.

▶ The designer has added variety to the muted colour scheme with floral cushions and a matching seat for the piano stool.

▶ There is new lighting to ensure that the room is bright enough for practising music.

AFTER

↑ Gaynor had said she wasn't keen on animal motifs but the designer did include one tile that featured a dog.

← Cushions and a throw add warmth to the neutral sofa.

JUDGE'S VIEW
This room is calm, elegant and right on brief. The curtains are very clever: although they're made from an inexpensive fabric, there is lots of it so as to feel luxurious. But the blue is a little too much for me.'

IDEAS FOR FEATURE WALLS p.91

CASE STUDY | A Dream Come True

Girls dream of being able to design their own bedroom – and this nine-year-old had all her wishes granted.

BRIEF

Gaynor wanted a makeover for the bedroom of her nine-year-old daughter, Rosie. It was a good opportunity to provide her with a room that would see her through her teens. Rosie was keen to stick with a girly theme – she liked pinks, purples, butterflies, hearts and gingham. She was also a huge bookworm and was keen to have lots of lighting so that she could read in bed. Storage and a desk were on the must-have list, and she was also hoping for some new curtains.

BEFORE

Bright colours

→ Shelving built in to the alcove provides plenty of space for Rosie's collection of books and other treasures.

Luxe fabrics

▶ Pale pink paint contrasts with a dramatic feature wall and matching curtains.

▶ Purple accents have also been added with a bedspread, a reupholstered balloon-back chair and cushions.

▶ The lighting is adjustable so that Rosie has good light to read by in bed and while sitting in her luxurious, grown-up chair.

▶ Cleverly concealed brackets make it appear as if the two piles of books on the wall are suspended in mid-air.

← Different coloured accents have been added using lampshades and a comfy beanbag.

↓ The bed now has a padded headboard for extra luxury – a room fit for a tween.

AFTER

JUDGE'S VIEW
'This must be every little girl's dream – and I think any trendy teenager wouldn't mind a room like this, either. The use of emerald green against the purple makes it very sophisticated, while on a practical level there's a nice new bed, lots of shelves and a rather beautiful fitted wardrobe.'

CHOOSING AND USING COLOURS p.33

CASE STUDY | Nicely Stripy

The family needed a playroom that doubled as a guest room but gave their designer free rein to come up with a scheme that would work.

BRIEF

The guest room was a blank canvas and a great size and shape. It was being used as both a playroom for the two children and a spare room for guests, and it had to remain a dual-purpose room that could be converted into a stylish space for guests when necessary – either using the day bed, that was already in the room or perhaps with a new double bed or sofa bed. Gaynor was happy for the room to become more grown up in style. She and Andrew were open to colour and pattern choices, provided the room was tasteful and practical.

BEFORE

Colour and texture

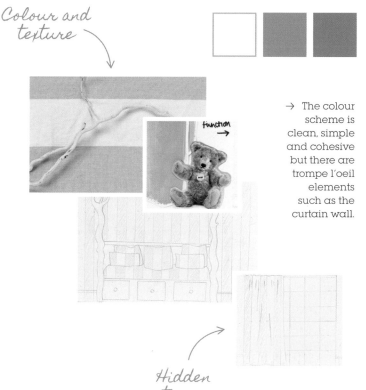

function →

→ The colour scheme is clean, simple and cohesive but there are trompe l'oeil elements such as the curtain wall.

Hidden storage

↓ The day bed looks elegant with a new cover and matching cushions.

▶ At first glance this appears to be a grown-up guestroom, but the white-painted trees give the room a fairytale element that hints at its other purpose as a playroom.

▶ Next to the window the curtained-off wall conceals storage for toys.

▶ A peg rail provides a place for guests to hang their clothes without the need for a wardrobe.

▶ Floor-length curtains and a soft blue rug give the room a luxurious feel.

▶ A painted box provides additional storage and also matches the colour scheme.

▶ A side table with a lamp doubles as a bedside table for guests.

AFTER

JUDGE'S VIEW

'It's dramatic but, because of the restful colours, there's a sense of peacefulness here, too. The trees are really fabulous – they add a magical feel. This room is fun, but with a grown-up edge.'

KEEPING KIDS' KIT IN CHECK p.130

CASE STUDY | Monochrome Magic

Even people with an eye for design and a house packed full of original features sometimes need a helping hand, especially when their home is spread over four levels.

BRIEF

Jim and Tracy had lived in their four-storey Georgian terrace for eight years. When they researched the history of the house they found it had had a colourful past: it had been a brothel and later a women's shelter. They had renovated most of their home in a chic and quirky style, but felt there was still room for improvement, with a number of unfinished spaces. They wanted to update the hallway, the front dining room, the guest bedroom and their oldest son's bedroom. The brief for the hallway was for it to be pale and welcoming, with a flat, matte paint finish – and definitely nothing too 'blingy'.

BEFORE

lower   line   Upper

Striped paint effect for walls

Stair runner

marble topped side table

↑ For each room the designer's proposal includes watercolour sketches, paint swatches and descriptions of ideas.

JUDGE'S VIEW
'The broad stripes address
the architecture, while the
demi lune table creates a
focal point. There are some
quirky bits of interest in
a space that's usually
just an ordinary
thoroughfare.'

▶ The dramatic floor tiles in the hallway provided inspiration for the scheme.

▶ Stripes of colour along the walls have created a modern dado rail; this effect continues up the stairs.

▶ The house is packed full of pieces from second-hand shops and antiques markets, including a statue of the Virgin Mary. The designer has also added a marble-topped demi lune table as a focal point.

▶ The pendant light shade is a witty, modern take on a chandelier.

→ The old carpet on the stairs has been replaced by a luxury runner with herringbone edging.

AFTER

← The hallway is now a bright and welcoming space that showcases some of the family's quirky pieces.

FINISHING
TOUCHES p.228

CASE STUDY | Tradition With a Twist

The challenge for this room was to transform it from an occasional dining room and dumping ground into a useful space for working, eating and relaxing.

BRIEF

The front dining room was used for entertaining at Christmas; for the rest of the year it was a dumping ground. Tracy wanted Jim to have somewhere to work from home, but the room also had to be a multi-functional space that could be used by all the family. The couple were slightly at odds over the décor, with Jim favouring clean lines and Japanese influences, while Tracy wanted a cool, eclectic gentleman's room with grey walls. The piano, sofa and books had to work within the design, but the couple wanted the dining table to be replaced with something more versatile.

BEFORE

Old desk and alcove shelving

Custom-made chair

→ The traditional dining set has been replaced by a snooker table with a custom-made cover that can be folded back, and a set of old school chairs.

▶ Glass shelving shows off Jim's precious book collection to its best advantage.

▶ A roll top desk in the alcove provides a place to work that has the benefit of natural light.

▶ Another custom made piece created using copper piping, the ceiling light is an industrial-style take on a chandelier.

▶ Tracy and Jim's wonderful antique sofa still has pride of place under the windows.

▶ The wall sconce complements the wealth of period features in the room.

← The designer commissioned this original chair; a local saddler made the leather seat.

AFTER

↑ The lion's head door knockers attached to the fire surround provides somewhere to store snooker cues.

JUDGE'S VIEW
'This is quite special. Before, this room had no purpose, and now it has the look of a games room. Maybe it's a little bit too themed. Sometimes less is more, but for design details it's top marks.'

CASE STUDY | Room for a Big Boy

Insect and building enthusiast Charlie needed a room that worked around his interests: he got all that and more.

BRIEF

Tracy and Jim's seven-year-old son Charlie had his bedroom on the top floor. Tracy was keen for his room to help showcase his interests – building and bugs – and allow his personality to flourish. She liked the idea of an industrial-style room that made use of an old school locker she had found in a charity shop. Charlie wanted a new bunk bed and Tracy was keen for him to have a bespoke concept that was quirky and practical for sleepovers with friends. Charlie also needed a new desk, new lighting and a low level table for his Lego and wooden structures.

BEFORE

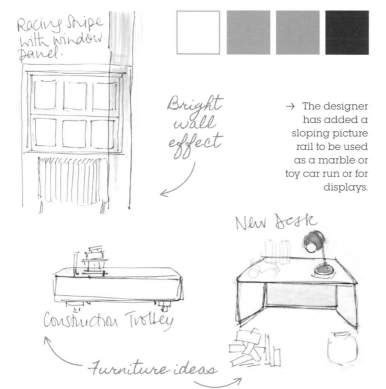

Racing stripe with window panel.

Bright wall effect

Construction Trolley

New Desk

Furniture ideas

→ The designer has added a sloping picture rail to be used as a marble or toy car run or for displays.

▶ The designer has kept the room bright and white but has added pops of colour into the scheme in a way that Charlie will find interesting.

▶ The customised bunk bed meets the brief and is a fun place to sleep, either on the top or the bottom.

▶ A simple white desk has been painted green underneath to tie in with the scheme.

▶ The storage box has a hole in the lid so that toys can be tidied away without disturbing what is on top.

← The old school locker has been upcycled and is now used for storing toys.

↓ Next to the bed Perspex cubes display Charlie's Lego creations and his collection of bugs.

AFTER

JUDGE'S VIEW
'It's really funky and original. The green stripe makes this space look so modern, and I love the slope for the toy cars. The flat-pack bunk bed has been completely modified with the front panel, and the pop of apple green inside makes it a really trendy little nook. I'm very impressed.'

CASE STUDY Blue Beauty

This room was a pure white box waiting to be given an injection of colour and 18th-century personality.

BRIEF

The spare bedroom was compact, with a double cast-iron bed and a chaise longue, and was often used by visiting grandparents. It was a blank canvas with original wooden floorboards, white walls, a white roller blind and a chandelier. Tracy and Jim were happy to give the designer a free rein, and were open to the room being repainted and carpeted. Some storage was needed, but they did not mind whether this was freestanding or built in. New lighting was also an option.

BEFORE

Side table

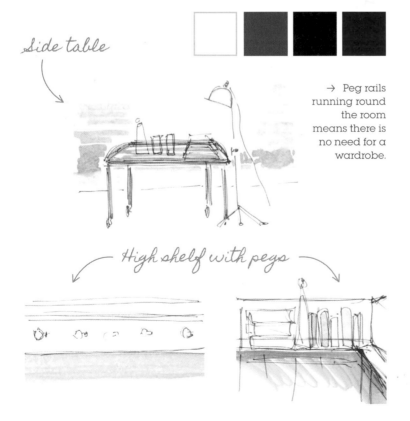

→ Peg rails running round the room means there is no need for a wardrobe.

High shelf with pegs

▶ The dramatic blue below the picture rail contrasts with the white above and the painted white floor.

▶ In a narrow room space is a a premium. The designer has taken out the chaise longue leaving more space to showcase the cast-iron bed.

▶ A high shelf provides valuable storage for Tracy's collection of finds as well as a place to hang clothes.

▶ The bedspread and floral cushions provide warmth and interest to the scheme.

▶ The floor light can be adjusted for reading in bed.

← An old table features a display of family photographs and a vintage-style milk jug.

AFTER

JUDGE'S VIEW

'If you were coming to stay for a weekend, you'd feel really at home here. The shelf and peg rail is a great idea for spare rooms that you don't want to clog up with wardrobes and chests of drawers. But I liked the room more when it was simple and pared back. For me, there's one too many knick-knacks.'

COLOUR KNOW-
HOW p.29

The big picture

In this section we take a look at your home as a whole: how to make the most of your space (however large or small), your range of choices for wallcoverings and flooring, ways to enhance every room with clever lighting, essential suggestions for all-important storage and tips for tackling technology. We also examine those harder-to-handle rooms: kitchens and bathrooms, with lots of practical pointers and inspirational ideas for both design and decoration.

Make the most of your space

No matter how big or small your home, it's time to maximise every square inch, creating a comfortable sense of space and using every room to its full potential.

In any home, large or tiny, the best spaces are those which are harmoniously clutter-free – practical rooms, easy and enjoyable to use every day, and good-looking to boot. Even large rooms suffer if you haven't sorted out adequate storage, if the furniture is badly arranged, or if the lighting is inadequate. The smaller the room, the more noticeable these problems become, and there is no doubt that tiny spaces require even more careful planning than usual.

That said, just because a room is small or awkwardly shaped, it doesn't mean that it can't be great. With pleasant proportions, the right colours and a shrewd choice of furnishings, you can turn a tiny or a tricky room into a wonderful gem.

There are two ways of dealing with problematic rooms: by altering them physically, or by using visual tricks to make them appear bigger, smaller, higher, lower, longer or wider.

Physical solutions

▶ Consider the big options – knocking through, raising the ceiling, adding a mezzanine, for example.

▶ Conventional hinged doors take up a lot of space in a small room. Can you swap them for sliding or bi-fold doors? Or you could remove the door entirely.

▶ Clear every bit of clutter you possibly can. Then sort out your storage. High-level storage can be the answer when space is tight.

▶ Folding, stacking, hideaway, compact and dual-purpose furniture are all good space-saving options.

↑ Vertical stripes can emphasise ceiling height in a tall room or give the illusion of space in a room with a lower ceiling.

STORAGE p.124

▶ If possible, fit underfloor heating and get rid of space-guzzling radiators.

▶ In rooms with low ceilings, replace dangling pendant lights with inset spots or table lamps.

Visual tricks

▶ In narrow rooms, fake a feeling of width by using horizontal patterns on walls or floors. Similarly, vertical stripes can make low-ceilinged rooms appear taller. A dark ceiling makes an overly high ceiling seem lower.

▶ In a small room, use the same colour on the walls, floors and ceiling. Blurring those boundaries increases the feeling of space.

▶ Light-reflecting paints are an inexpensive way to boost a sense of space.

▶ Being able to see more of the floor makes a room seem less crowded, so use wall-hung furniture in appropriate places.

▶ Furniture on slender legs also shows more floor space – giving the illusion of a larger area. The same goes for anything made from glass or acrylic.

▶ Use mirrors and other reflective surfaces as much as possible in a small or dark room.

↑→ Create a workspace in an area that might otherwise be wasted. Folding chairs can be put away when not in use, saving masses of space.

Fitting in a home office

We all need a workspace somewhere at home, whether you work from home full time or are simply answering the odd email. As long as you can find room for a small desk (or even a shelf in an alcove, set at the right height) with some storage and a plug socket or two nearby, you are well on your way. Here are some ideas:

▶ Under the stairs.

▶ In the loft.

▶ In a large cupboard.

▶ On the landing.

▶ In a spare bedroom.

▶ A corner of the bedroom, living room or kitchen.

▶ The garage or garden shed.

▶ A dedicated building in the garden.

Zoning and flow

Don't take your home for granted. With some clever thinking you can configure your space so that it suits you and your family perfectly.

When it comes to thinking about how we use our homes, designers might talk about zoning and flow, but what's important is this: how does your house suit you and your family? Is it easy or awkward to live in?

Start by considering the house as a whole, trying to see each room as a blank canvas. Are you really making the best use of the layout? Sometimes we follow preconceived ideas, or those imposed on the house by previous owners, when really we need to change things around – turn a spare bedroom into a home office, or make a seldom-used dining room a teenagers' hangout. It could make sense to put a laundry room near the bedrooms rather than in its traditional place by the kitchen, or turn a first-floor bedroom into a sitting room to make the most of lovely views.

Old houses can be more spacious than new-builds, but do offer particular challenges as they can often be a warren of small rooms, rarely have enough bathrooms and never have enough plug sockets. Can you convert a box room into an ensuite? If you extended across a side return, could you create a family-friendly open-plan living space? And what will happen if you have a baby, your children leave home, an elderly relative comes to stay, or you change career and need a fully functioning home office? If possible, future-proof your home so that it's flexible enough to deal with whatever life throws at it.

If the big projects (extensions, loft conversions, going open-plan) are not possible or necessary, there are plenty of smaller changes that can help streamline your home. Such relatively simple alterations as re hanging a door, moving a radiator, enlarging a window or adding wall lights and extra plug sockets can turn an awkward home into one that's tailor-made for you. Make the effort now – you definitely won't regret it.

PLANNING MAKES PERFECT p.54

Designing a room layout

▶ Measure the room as carefully as possible, and draw a scaled-down plan of it (as if you were looking from above) on graph paper. Draw in the current positions of windows, doors, built-in cupboards, radiators, plug sockets and light fittings.

▶ Think about whether all the architectural elements are in the right place. Perhaps it would help if you took down a wall, moved a radiator, re-hung the door so it opens the other way, or added some extra plug sockets?

▶ If you are working on a bathroom or kitchen, work out where the pipes run. Will you need to alter them?

▶ On a separate sheet of paper, but using the same scale as the room plan, sketch the approximate shape of your furniture (again, as if you were looking at them from above). Cut them out and place them on the plan. Do they fit well into the space? Is there enough 'activity room' around them (space to swing your legs out of bed; elbow room around a basin)?

▶ Move the furniture around or re-assess its shape and size as necessary. Once everything is in the right place, you should have the basics of a functional and comfortable room.

↑ Grouping the furniture at one end of this long room creates a cosy space for relaxing.

← Open plan kitchen/dining spaces are perfect for families and entertaining.

Access all areas

There's no doubt that huge, airy and bright open-plan spaces are wonderfully appealing. But just how do you create the perfect open-plan, multi-use, family-friendly space?

❶ If you work from home or really value your privacy, then keep at least one living space where you can shut yourself away. Alternatively, folding doors, or a simple screen, could do the trick.

❷ When creating an open-plan kitchen, dining and living area, you will either need a separate utility room or a super-quiet dishwasher and washing machine. A low-decibel extractor over the cooker is vital, too.

❸ In any room that has more than one function, the furniture needs to blend from one area to another. Create an overall style that works as well for comfy seating as it does for kitchen units.

❹ Delineate areas within the open-plan space by varying paint colours and using clever lighting – different circuits are best, controlled by switches or dimmers.

❺ Either 'zone' different areas by varying the flooring, or go for an all-purpose hard or vinyl floor that can be softened with rugs where necessary.

❻ Open-plan rooms have less wall space for storage, so you have to be clever with your clobber. Consider open shelves that double as a room divider, seating that doubles as storage and fitted furniture that uses every inch of height or quirky corner that you have.

❼ Open-plan, multi-purpose rooms can lack focus. A feature wall or large work of art may be the answer.

❽ Conventional furniture can look out of place in a large, open space – you may need to buy larger-than-average pieces.

↑ This large living space is divided into living, dining, play and work areas.

→ The carpet and paint colours make the two areas of this long, thin room co-ordinate seamlessly.

↓ A stylish lighting scheme and careful placement of furniture separates the living and dining areas in this room.

Connecting spaces

Halls and landings often get overlooked, yet your hall is like a handshake: the introduction to your house, while the landing is a vital linking area. Think of both as if they were rooms in their own right, and give them the attention they deserve.

Increase the feeling of space in a narrow hallway by using pale colours and large mirrors. Keep the space as clear as possible by adding slim storage furniture, hung on walls where possible. Welcoming lighting that leads the eye into your home is important. Avoid wall lights as they can be obstacles, but think pretty chandeliers or perhaps a series of contemporary recessed ceiling lights. Even on the smallest landing you can use walls to display art or photographs, or maybe hang a set of slender bookshelves. In a slightly larger area you could have a small ottoman, a trunk or even a handy desk, tallboy or chest of drawers. Bright lights are important so that you don't trip on the stairs. Lastly, make sure your landing's decorative scheme works well when doorways to other rooms are open.

Knocking down walls

Before you get out the sledgehammer, make sure that the wall you are knocking down isn't loadbearing. If it is, you will have to insert a beam over the new opening (employ a structural engineer to do the calculations). Either way, you must also check with your local planning authority whether the work is subject to building regulations.

FINDING A GOOD BUILDER p.57

Walls

From the simplest of painted walls to vibrant wallpaper or complex tiling, the right wall finish adds atmosphere and creates character. in a room.

A plain white wall is not the most exciting decorative idea. However, it could actually be just the thing to show off a colourful collection, or provide a counterpoint to brightly patterned upholstery. Choosing the best wall finish for your space is all about context – and is just as important in terms of decorative effect as selecting colours, fabrics and furnishings. A change of wallcovering can transform cold into cosy, boring into beautiful and out-of-date into ultra cool.

As well as personal choice, there is a practical element, too. While some finishes are delicate, others can protect your walls from bumps, knocks, scrapes, sticky fingers and muddy paws. Some finishes look their best on perfectly straight, smooth walls; others are great at hiding blemishes. Prepare your walls properly and then find your perfect finish. You'll be spoilt for choice.

Preparing your walls

Before you decorate, make sure the surface of your wall is as smooth as possible. The better your preparation, the better the final results. If there is old wallpaper on the walls, it should be stripped off prior to preparing the plaster. Only keep it if it is okay to paint over it. Once stripped, cut out and replace any bulging, loose or crumbling plaster. If you have new plaster it must be properly dried out and, before painting, primed with watered-down emulsion. If you plan to wallpaper over new plaster, you will also need to paint it with sizing solution or watered-down wallpaper paste. If you hang lining paper (go horizontally; it's called cross-lining) it will help to disguise lumpy, bumpy walls before painting or wallpapering.

↓ This large stick-on mural adds to the period feel in this Regency living room.

Ideas for feature walls

Roller patterns

With some patience and a steady hand you can create your own wallpaper using patterned paint rollers for a truly individual look.

Bold and beautiful

Wallpaper with an oversized pattern and vivid colours may well be too much for a whole room, but makes a great focal point on just one wall.

All stuck up

Transform your wall with peel-off stickers. They come in all sorts of divine designs from simple shapes to complex illustrations.

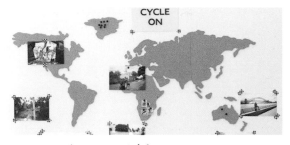

Map of the world

Large maps (old or new) are attractive and educational. Simply paste straight on to the wall. Try sheet music and wrapping paper, too.

Frame wall

Group vintage frames, mirrors and even graphic letters, in all shapes and sizes, to create an intriguing and eye-catching focal point.

Pick up a paintbrush

Try modern, graphic ideas such as bold stripes running horizontally or vertically around the room.

DISPLAYS ON WALLS
p.222

Wallpaper

Fashionable and fun, wallpaper can be subtle and chic or full of impact. There is a world of wallpaper choice out there, including not only conventional machine-printed designs, but also natural woven fibres, light-reflecting metallic papers and waterproof vinyls.

If you are looking for something a little different: there are hand-finished papers that feature cut-work, stitching and appliqué; interactive papers that you can colour in or add stickers to; expensive hand-blocked papers; three-dimensional designs incorporating crystals, beading, sequins and tiny LED lights; digitally printed papers made to your own design; and even magnetic wallpapers that work as noticeboards.

Convention has it that you hang the same type of wallpaper vertically all around a room. But who wants to follow convention? Create a feature by papering just one wall, or choose different colourways of the same pattern to use in different areas. You could even hang your wallpaper horizontally, or mix up the designs to create a handcrafted, bohemian effect.

Helpful hints

▶ Always buy enough paper to complete your project, allowing for pattern repeats and wastage.

▶ Check the batch numbers are the same on all the rolls to avoid slight colour variations, and use the paste recommended by the manufacturer.

▶ The heavier the paper, the easier it will be to hang and the longer it should last.

▶ Decorate the ceiling and all the woodwork before you start papering.

Types of wallpaper

▶ Standard decorative wallpapers are ideal for areas that don't suffer from moisture or severe wear and tear.

▶ Vinyls are durable and easy to apply (they often come pre-pasted). They are all-purpose, but especially suitable for kitchens and bathrooms. Some are textured.

▶ Washable wallpapers have a transparent coating, which means they can be wiped down.

▶ Embossed wallpapers feature a raised, textured pattern and are meant to be painted. Blown vinyls are similar.

▶ Flock wallpapers feature stencil-like designs with a velvety texture.

▶ Woodchip wallpaper contains tiny chips of wood and is usually painted.

▶ Foils are metallic wallcoverings that can vary from a gentle sheen to almost mirror-like.

▶ Natural wallcoverings include materials such as woven grass, silk, wood veneer, hessian and cork, backed with paper. They are often delicate and hard to clean.

Hanging wallpaper: where to start

Deciding where to start is important. If you begin at the short section of wall above the doorframe, you can disguise any pattern mismatch at the point where your last drop meets your first drop without it being noticeable. Or you can start in a corner, and work away from it in both directions. Centre large motifs over the most obvious focal point – a fireplace, above the bed or between two windows.

USING PATTERN
p.38

How to hang wallpaper

1 Once you have chosen your starting point (see below left), use a roll of paper to mark where the drops will fall around the room. Move the starting point a little if any joins are awkward.

2 Use a plumb line to mark a vertical line as a guide for the edge of the first drop of wallpaper. It's really important to get this right – if you start off wrong, your pattern will be uneven by the time you get to the end.

3 Cut a length of wallpaper, allowing enough for the drop plus about 10cm (4in) extra for trimming top and bottom. On a long, wipe-clean table, paste the paper with a wide brush, working from the centre outwards. When you reach the end of the table, gently fold the paper over, pasted side to pasted side, and continue pasting.

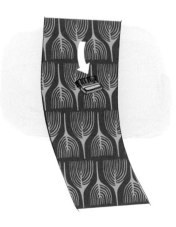

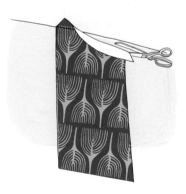

4 Hang the top section of paper, sliding it so the edge meets the line you marked and about 5cm (2in) overlaps onto the ceiling. Working from the middle, smooth down with a paperhanging brush.

5 Mark the trimming line at the top with a pencil or the back of a pair of scissors. Gently peel the top edge of paper away, cut off the excess along the line and brush the edge back onto the wall. Repeat at the bottom.

6 Before cutting the next drop, ensure it is long enough for you to match the pattern. Hang as before, making sure the edges join exactly. On flat papers, run a seam roller down the joins. Wipe off any excess paste with a damp sponge.

Paint

Nothing transforms a room as quickly and easily as a fresh coat of paint on the walls and woodwork.

A handy guide to paint

▶ Solvent-based paints take longer to dry and have a strong smell, but they flow beautifully and dry smoothly; brushes need cleaning with white spirit.

▶ Water-based paints are quick-drying, with a low odour, but are not generally as durable as oil-based versions; brushes are easily cleaned with water.

▶ Primer is used to seal a bare surface and help paint to adhere and give a good finish.

▶ Undercoat is applied on top of primer to give 'body' to gloss. It comes in different colours, depending on the shade of topcoat to be used.

▶ Emulsion is always water-based and usually comes in a matt or silk (shinier) finish. Use a brush, roller or paint pad to apply to walls and ceilings (see below right).

▶ Paint for woodwork and metal comes in a variety of finishes, including gloss, satin and eggshell. It may be oil- or water-based, and is suitable for interior and exterior. Non-drip and one-coat glosses are also available.

▶ Kitchen and bathroom paints usually have a sheen; they are scrubbable, can help with condensation problems and may include a fungicide.

▶ Masonry paints are smooth or textured, and designed for outdoor brickwork, stone, concrete, pebbledash and render.

▶ Eco paints, such as limewash are water-based and made with natural ingredients. They are 'breathable', which is important for porous walls.

▶ Specialist paints include radiator and floor paint, fire-retardant and anti-burglar paint, blackboard paint, damp-inhibiting paint, suede-effect and even magnetic paint.

Roller, pad or brush?

Rollers are the most popular. They cover large areas quickly, but may splash and can't reach into corners. They also leave an orange-peel surface, which some people hate. Wide brushes are a traditional choice, but are slower and require skill to achieve a really good effect. Pads make the paint smooth and even, but can spread it too thinly, meaning you need more coats.

How to paint your walls

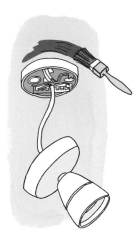

1 Before you start, turn off the power supply and unscrew ceiling rose covers and the faceplates of sockets and switches so you that can paint behind them. Vacuum throughout the room to avoid dust settling on wet paint, and cover furnishings and the floor.

2 Paint the ceiling first, starting in a corner near the window. If you can't reach the ceiling easily, use a long-handled roller or a stepladder. Use a small brush to paint a 5cm (2in) band around all the edges – you can overlap onto the walls a little, as you will 'cut in' later with your wall colour. Choose a roller sleeve with the correct fibre type and pile length for your paint and wall surface.

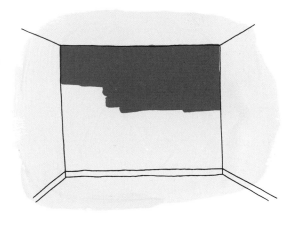

3 Going from the wet edges you have just painted, roll overlapping strokes in all directions, in bands about 60cm (23½in) wide. Start near a window so that the light on the surface shows any patches that have been missed. Reload the sleeve and apply a little further away from where you have just painted, and then blend.

4 For the walls, start by cutting in at a top corner. Then, with the roller, work downwards in bands. If you are right-handed you will find it easier to work from right to left and vice versa if you are left-handed. Finish a whole wall at a time so that areas do not dry before you blend them in, this can give a blotchy effect.

CHOOSING AND USING COLOURS p.33

Tiles

Just like wallpaper, tiles come in a fabulous variety of colours and patterns – and can be used in all sorts of ways around your home.

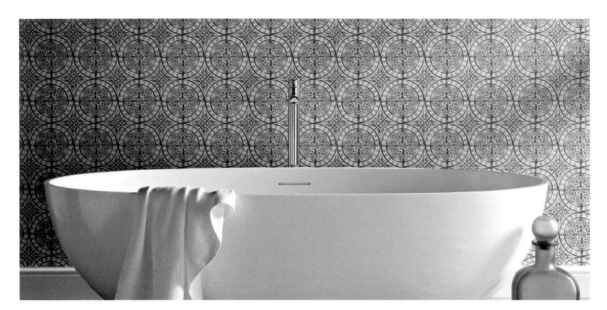

Tiles can be sleek and machine-made or rustic and hand-made; shiny and glazed or matt and unglazed; perfectly smooth or nicely textured; even digitally printed with your own designs. Long-lasting and hard-wearing, waterproof and easy to clean, tiles are ideal as wall finishes for bathrooms, showers and behind kitchen worktops. They are also great for hallways, conservatories, laundry and utility rooms, and, given their immense decorative potential, can sometimes work as part of a living area, too.

The visual impact of a tiled area – whether it's a whole wall or a small splashback – depends on a number of factors, including colour, pattern and texture, as well as size (from huge slabs to tiny mosaic tiles) and shape (square and rectangular are most common, but other shapes are available). What also makes a huge difference is the layout you choose – a simple grid, offset (or brick bond), herringbone, pinwheel or random, whether you use borders or a mix of different tiles, how widely they are spaced and even the colour of your grout.

A quick guide to tiles

▶ **Ceramic tiles:** Relatively inexpensive, these don't need sealing or polishing and are easily wiped clean.

▶ **Porcelain tiles:** Heavier and more hardwearing than ceramic tiles, these can often be used outdoors as well as indoors. Surface effects include natural stone, metals, concrete, fabric, wood and leather.

▶ **Glass tiles:** These may be clear, frosted and coloured, and have a lovely translucent appearance.

▶ **Mosaics:** Small mosaic tiles are usually supplied on a backing sheet and used for decorative effect.

▶ **Natural stone tiles:** Limestone, marble, granite and slate are all natural stone tiles. They can be porous, and often need to be sealed before use.

↑ Stunning Turkish-style tiles can give a Mediterranean feel to a bathroom.

GLOBAL INFLUENCES p.10

How to tile a wall

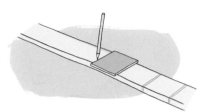

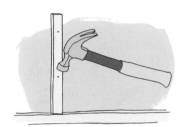

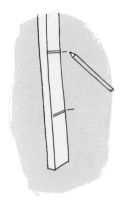

1 Make sure your surface is clean and dry. You can tile over existing tiles, as long as they are securely fixed. Mark up a length of wood to use as a tiling gauge, allowing for the gaps between the tiles as well. Always make sure you check your horizontal lines carefully.

2 'Set out' your tiled area. Find the centre of your wall and mark the position of the tiles from there. Adjust your starting point if you find you will end up cutting lots of thin slivers to fit around obstacles such as doors, windows or bathroom fittings. Ideally, you will have a border of cut tiles of the same width at the end of each row of tiles.

3 To support the tiles while the adhesive sets, temporarily fix battens (using part-driven masonry pins) along the wall, about half a tile height above the skirting board (depending on the setting out). Use a spirit level to check that they are horizontal. If you are tiling a large area, a vertical guide batten is also useful.

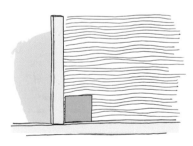

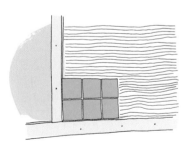

4 Apply the adhesive to the wall with a toothed spreader, drawing it evenly across the wall. Use enough to fix about 10 or 12 tiles. Bed the first tile into place with a slight twist, using the battens as a guide.

5 Add a tile spacer, then press the second tile into place, and so on, until you have completed the bottom row. Carry on spreading adhesive and adding rows until all the whole tiles are in place.

6 Cut tiles to fit the gaps, spread adhesive on their backs and push into place. Wait for the adhesive to set, then remove the tile spacers and battens, and tile in the space below your bottom row. Wait until this is dry and then fill the joints with grout.

Other wallcoverings

Paint and wallpaper are not the only ways to cover a wall: with a little imagination and ingenuity, almost any flat surface can be employed to create an interesting decorative effect.

↑ Original brickwork can be treated in different ways and gives an industrial feel to a space.

Types of wallcoverings

Mirror

A wall (or a portion of it) covered with a sheet of mirror will reflect light around and instantly make the room seem bigger.

Fabric

This is a traditional-looking, expensive technique that is great for insulating against cold and noise.

Leather

Unusual and expensive, leather walls add luxurious character, soften sounds and are even fire-retardant. Leather develops a patina over time.

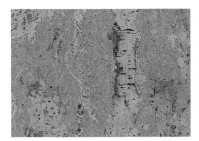

Cork

Warm and soft to the touch, eco-friendly, insulating and soundproofing, cork sheets or tiles offer many appealing qualities.

Composites and laminates

Sheets of plastic laminate or solid composite waterproof and need few joins; they are a good choice for bathrooms.

Sheet metal

Sheets of metal (steel, copper, aluminium) can be used to create an unusual wall installation. They can be textured, laser-cut and even rusty.

Polished plaster

Also known as Venetian plaster, this old Italian technique involves applying several thin coats of plaster and polishing with wax. The effect can be like marble, stone or suede.

Timber panelling

Panelling can hide uneven walls and is a great insulator. It also has warmth and character. Fielded panelling gives a classic effect, while tongue and groove is cosy and gives a country feel.

Thames Tunnel Mill
Rotherhithe 1843

The River Thames and the former docklands of East London were once the beating heart of industrial Britain. In the 19th century, Rotherhithe was transformed from unused marshland to bustling industrial hub as land was turned into docks to cope with ships bringing in goods such as timber from Scandinavia, Canada and the Baltics. This trade gave rise to place names like Canada Water, Baltic Quay and Helsinki Square.

The expanding Victorian Empire of the mid-1800s also played a part in bringing new goods to the docklands. The Thames Tunnel Mill, constructed in the 1860s, ground tapioca imported from the West Indies and rice and maize from the Americas for more than 100 years.

But by 1969, the shipping trade was using container vessels too large to navigate the shallow, silted waters of the Thames, and the Docklands went into decline, its warehouses abandoned and left to ruin. The Thames Tunnel Mill closed in 1972.

In 1981 the Thatcher Government set up the London Docklands Development Corporation to help restore some of the Dockland's former glory. The Thames Tunnel Mill was one of the area's earliest regeneration projects, and was used to show private developers that this part of East London was worthy of investment. It worked, and between 1981 and 1998 24,000 homes were built in the Docklands as part of the largest redevelopment project in Europe.

← An image of the Thames Tunnel Mill from 1937; it remained in operation until 1972.

→ Very few old buildings in Rotherhithe have remained. The Thames Tunnel Mill is one of only a handful that survive – a true monument to the area's industrial past.

▶ The Thames Tunnel Mill was one of the first industrial buildings to be converted in Britain. Only the façade of the Grade II listed building with its iron windows was retained – the heart of the original building was completely gutted.

▶ The cavernous space was converted into 70 small apartments across six floors.

▶ Rooms were built around each of the windows to let in as much light as possible, and in the end not a single window was bricked over.

▶ The industrial-type windows have two sections and were designed for maximum ventilation: both panes swivel.

▶ Warehouse conversions come in all shapes and sizes – carving up big industrial spaces comes with individual challenges and difficulties. Mezzanine levels are popular in some conversions, large open plan rooms in others.

▶ As this development was originally built as social housing, most of the flats were designed as one-bedroom apartments.

CASE STUDY French Country Living

Pale, neutral colours on walls and floors, a pretty mix of fabrics and refurbished vintage furniture give this living room a breath of French air.

BRIEF

Anna wanted a comfortable room in a French-influenced style that was good for entertaining – her lack of seating meant that her large sofa often became a bit crowded. She had acquired a number of pieces of vintage furniture that she had not yet been able to restore and needed help to bring them back to life. She was keen to see some colour on the walls, but favoured a neutral scheme rather than brights. She wanted to replace her stark lighting with floor or table lamps, and although the floor was in good condition, she thought a rug would soften the look.

BEFORE

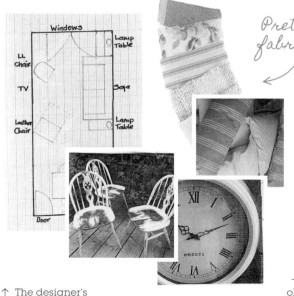

Pretty fabrics

↑ The designer's proposal incorporates Anna's existing furniture within the new scheme for the room.

→ Anna's old leather armchair has been restored and recovered.

JUDGE'S VIEW
'There's a beautiful look
here where there wasn't
one before. But I'm getting
South of France rather
than Parisian chic.'

↓ Rearranging the
seating and adding table
lamps either side of the
sofa makes the room feel
much more welcoming.

▶ A soft, neutral rug has softened the wooden floor.

▶ The two blinds over the balcony windows mean that the doors can be opened easily.

▶ A variety of cushions add colour and comfort to Anna's large sofa.

▶ The designer has painted the table legs bright blue to add a splash of colour; the distressed chairs add an element of shabby chic to the elegant room.

▶ A wall-mounted TV means that technology does not fight with the style of the room.

↓ A shelving unit on
the back wall gives
a place for Anna to
display her colourful
glassware.

AFTER

↑ Ornaments and artwork
bring in a rainbow of colour.

UPCYCLED
FURNITURE AND
ACCESSORIES p.185

CASE STUDY Boat-house Style

This functional yet tired space was given an overhaul to reflect the homeowner's rustic style and love of the river, as well as solving his storage issues.

BRIEF

Artist Ricardo wanted to maximise his river view with a boathouse-inspired living and dining room that incorporated natural materials, rope, wood and ladders. His main problem was a pair of built-in cupboards, used as a workstation and for storage, which he felt were overly dominating. He wanted to replace them with a more subtle storage solution – something that would open up the room and make the most of the space. If possible Ricardo also wanted to sandblast the paint off the brick walls and replace the lino with a real wood floor that would also be in keeping with the boathouse theme.

BEFORE

→ The designer's beautifully presented mood board includes samples, photographs and a detailed floor plan.

Brick walls

Wooden floor

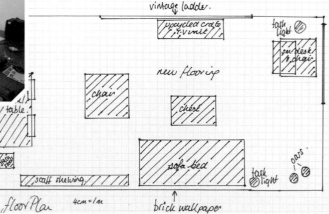

▶ An old ladder mounted on the wall provides an original way to display Ricardo's maritime pieces.

▶ The windows now have wooden shutters that allow the maximum of light into the room when they are not being used.

▶ Smart new flooring provides a shiny surface that contrasts well with matt paintwork and the suede sofa cover.

▶ The industrial-style chair provides some stylish additional seating.

▶ Touches of wood and rope continue the maritime theme throughout the whole room.

→ Old maps have been used to cover tins to store pens and other useful items.

↓ The chest used as a coffee table also doubles as storage.

AFTER

↑ The wooden shelving has been cleverly angled to make the most of the wall space.

→ The fitted wardrobes have been replaced with a useful workspace.

DESIGN HIGHLIGHT

↗ The striking wallpaper has a slight texture and was a quicker and less expensive way to create the effect of exposed-brickwork that Ricardo wanted. The judges were initially dubious, but in the end felt that it really worked in the scheme.

SETTING UP A HOME OFFICE p.133

JUDGE'S VIEW
'What a nice feeling in this room.
The boat-house look is spot on the
brief. But there is absolutely no hidden
storage. It's styled beautifully, but is
it really practical?'

← The wire light
fitting on a long
lead can be
moved around
the room.

→ The upcycled
apple crates provide
both a TV unit and
additional storage.

CASE STUDY | An African Dream

By adding colour, pattern, light and some ingenious storage solutions, this cluttered, mismatched room became a stylish, African-themed retreat.

BRIEF

Angela had lived at Thames Tunnel Mills for 20 years; she had recently moved from a studio into a one-bedroom apartment and was not sure how to decorate the extra space. She wanted an African-inspired room, fusing natural woods and exotic fabrics. Lighting and storage were the key elements she wanted to see incorporated into ther living room, which was also used for eating and working. The flooring was in poor condition and was something Angela was keen to see replaced. She also wanted a sofa bed for guests to use. Angela loved every shade of green, but she also liked red, orange, yellow and brown; she was also keen to see bold use of pattern.

Colourful flowers

African fabrics

African artefacts

BEFORE

→ The designer's proposal shows a mixture of bold colour, patterned fabric, African influence and retro furniture.

▶ Three walls are painted in a cool, concrete-like grey, to balance the vivid colours used elsewhere.

▶ The new flooring gives the room a sleek, polished look.

▶ A blind hung high over the window lets in the maximum amount of light.

▶ The retro sideboard gives Angela her much-needed storage and is a beautiful piece of furniture.

▶ Brightly coloured cushions in bold patterns decorate the neutral colour of the sofa bed.

→ The new cushion covers fit the theme perfectly without being predictable.

↓ The upcycled apple crates are a great storage solution and fit neatly into a corner.

↓ Framed African art has been used to brighten up one section of the neutral wall.

AFTER

BLINDS
p.220

DESIGN HIGHLIGHT

↓ The coffee table doubles up as a playground for Angela's beloved cats.

↓ The shelves in mixed woods break up the neutral wall and mean that Angela does not have to lose precious floor space with freestanding shelving.

→ The fitted cupboards have been given some colourful new handles.

↑ Now the TV is wall mounted it no longer dominates the room.

JUDGE'S VIEW

'Angela's pieces were lost in here, but now they are a really nice centrepiece. The designer has thought of everything.'

ACCESSORIES
p.202

Project

The designers at Thames Tunnel Mill were each given two old apple crates to incorporate into their design; these can be made into inexpensive shelving.

Planters to create a window box.

A media unit with storage.

A cleverly grouped storage solution.

HOW TO MAKE SHELVES OUT OF APPLE CRATES

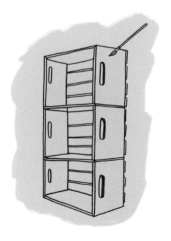

1 First clean your crates and sand them to give an even surface that won't cause splinters. Using brackets and short screws, screw the crates together at the back on each side.

2 Turn the crates on their long side and use small nails to fix the front of each crate to the one underneath.

3 You can leave the wood natural, or apply paint or varnish.

Floors

From soft wool to warm wood, classic carpet to fashionable rubber, flooring is fundamental to the look and feel of a room.

These days, almost anything goes for flooring: gone are the days of tiles in the kitchen, carpet in the bedroom and floorboards in the living room – you can have mosaic in your living room, rubber in your kitchen and marble in your home office, if you so wish. Before aesthetics though, it comes down to practicalities – the amount of wear and tear the floor will take. So put your toughest, most durable flooring in the hall and living room, and a more delicate type in a spare bedroom, for example. For kitchens, bathrooms, utility rooms and conservatories, there is another consideration: how well it will withstand spills, splashes and general humidity. Choose the right flooring for your space and it will not only look good but also last and last.

What lies beneath

The success of any flooring depends on the sub-floor underneath. For example, if you lay carpets and sheet flooring, such as vinyl or lino, straight onto floorboards, after a while you will begin to see the parallel lines showing through. You need to cover the boards first with a thin sheet of hardboard or plywood. (What's more, a good quality underlay makes a huge difference to how long carpet will last.) If you plan to lay heavy stone tiles, the sub-floor may need reinforcing – if in doubt check with your builder or a structural engineer. Tiles of any type are best laid onto a dry, smooth, level, concrete sub-floor – you can apply a self-levelling compound, if necessary.

Types of flooring

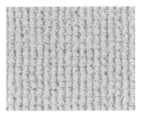

Carpet

Warm, soft and quiet underfoot, carpet is a classic choice. The downside is that stains can be hard to remove.

Natural fibres

Sisal, coir, jute, seagrass and rush all come under this heading. They are available in a range of colours, weaves and textures.

Vinyl

Available in both sheet and tile form, vinyl is relatively easy to lay. Warm and soft underfoot; it is also water-resistant.

Linoleum

Modern lino is durable, stain-resistant and easy to clean, as well as being environmentally friendly.

Solid wood

Timeless and durable, solid wood flooring (boards or parquet) is extremely practical, although it is not a cheap option.

Laminate floors

Varies from inexpensive – a photo of wood bonded to a chipboard base – to quality 'engineered' versions.

Ceramic and porcelain

Heat- and water-resistant, durable and easy to clean, but this flooring is cold underfoot.

Stone and slate

Sandstone, limestone, slate and granite are all luxurious choices. They can be porous, so check whether they require sealing.

Bamboo

Fast-growing and self-regenerating, bamboo is environmentally friendly and easy to clean. It is good for humid areas, too.

Marble

The epitome of luxury, with a beautiful grain and attractive colouring. But it is cold and hard underfoot.

Rubber

In the form of tiles or sheets, rubber is warm and soft, yet durable and water-resistant. A textured design gives better grip.

Leather

Expensive and unusual, leather floors require regular buffing or waxing and develop a patina over the years.

Wood

Wooden floors are beautiful, hardwearing and just get better and better as they age.

Solid wood

Wooden flooring is available as boards in a variety of widths, strips (less than 10cm/4in wide), blocks (extremely strong, laid in patterns such as herringbone and basketweave) and parquet (like blocks, but thinner, see below). Oak and pine are classic, while beech, ash and maple are practical and attractive, too. Exotic hardwoods such as wenge, teak, merbau and iroko make a dramatic impression, while bamboo (technically a grass, but a sustainable alternative nevertheless) has an individual look. Solid wooden floors can be sanded, painted, limed, stained, waxed or varnished.

Engineered wood

This is sometimes called multi-layer or, confusingly, laminated wood, and is made either from several layers of solid timber or else a thin layer of solid timber attached to a cheaper base made from MDF, plywood, chipboard or softwood. Solid-wood engineered boards are cross-bonded for stability (meaning they won't warp or move, which solid timber is prone to), making them a good choice with underfloor heating.

Laminate

Made from a resin-impregnated decorative paper surface layer printed with photographs of real wood, bonded to a thin MDF or chipboard core. With cheaper versions it is easy to spot the pattern repeat, plus they're less durable. More expensive laminate flooring can be incredibly tough – look for a long guarantee.

Parquet

Originally a French 17th-century flooring technique, parquet became affordable (thanks to mechanisation) in the early 20th century and remained fashionable until the 1930s, when carpet and lino began to take precedence. Made up of hardwood blocks laid in a geometric pattern – such as herringbone, basketweave and chevron – parquet has a distinctive and timeless look.

How to sand floorboards

1 Mend or replace any damaged boards. Fill any large gaps with thin slivers of matching timber. Hammer any protruding nail heads below the surface of the board. Remove furniture and soft furnishings, seal the door and open the windows – there will be a lot of dust.

2 Use a drum sander fitted with coarse paper for the main floor area, sanding diagonally from corner to corner. Start with the drum tilted back off the floor, switch it on and then gently lower it down. Guide it in a slow, steady line. Don't allow it to stop, or it will gouge a hollow in your boards. At the end of the run, tilt it back, switch it off and let the drum stop before you lower it.

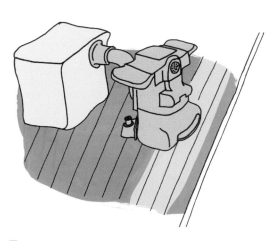

3 Work in parallel, slightly overlapping runs, and when you have finished the first diagonal, sweep up and then do the opposite diagonal. Sweep again, then change to medium sandpaper and work parallel to the boards. Use a fine grade sandpaper for a final, parallel sand.

4 Use a disc sander for the edges and corners, working from coarse to fine paper as before. A scraper or power drill sanding attachment will get into any areas the edging sander can't reach. Vaccuum, then finish by wiping the floor with a cloth dampened with white spirit.

Carpets and rugs

Soft and comfortable underfoot, carpets and rugs are both practical and beautiful, offering an almost unlimited choice of colour and pattern, and an enormous variety of textures.

↑ A rug can bring texture and a welcome splash of colour to a wooden floor.

↗ Rugs designed for children are colourful and fun, and soft for little feet.

What are carpets and rugs made of?

▶ **Wool:** Wool is warm and sumptuous, soft and durable, and does not soil easily.

▶ **Wool blends:** The most common blends are 80% wool with 20% nylon (often recommended as the ideal combination of softness and strength); 80% wool with 10% nylon and 10% polyester; and 50% wool with 50% polypropylene.

▶ **Nylon:** Extremely hardwearing, nylon also takes stain-resistant treatments well.

▶ **Polypropylene:** Resistant to stains and abrasions, polypropylene wears well and is good value for money.

▶ **Polyester:** Stain-resistant, light and bulky, polyester has a lustrous appearance.

Types of carpet pile

▶ **Loop:** The pile tufts are left uncut. Avoid if you have pets.

▶ **Cord:** The loops are pulled tight against the backing, giving a very low pile.

▶ **Saxony:** A deeper pile with a soft, sensuous feel and appearance.

▶ **Shag:** Extra-long pile – can catch high heels.

▶ **Twist:** A loop pile that uses yarn with a higher twist than usual to give a coarse, rugged surface. The best types twist two yarn ends tightly together for a very hardwearing carpet.

▶ **Velvet:** A sheared, short pile with a smooth, luxurious finish.

What carpet where?

Carpets are classified for light, moderate, general, heavy and extra heavy domestic use. Select a tough carpet for a hallway: perhaps an 80/20 (wool/nylon) twist classified for heavy domestic; while for a living room a combination of a luxury look with a robust performance, such as a loop or velvet pile, would be best. A spare bedroom carpet could be more delicate – a velvet or Saxony classified for light domestic use, for example. For a seamless look, lay carpet suitable for general use throughout. Carpets are inadvisable in kitchens, and best avoided in bathrooms.

Add colour and interest with a rug

A great starting point for a decorative scheme, rugs come in an infinite variety of shapes and sizes, textures and colours, patterns and prices. There is a wonderful range of hand-made rugs from around the world, including Indian dhurries, Greek flokatis, Middle Eastern kelims and French aubussons. Modern machine-made rugs can be very attractive, and you can even have a rug woven to your own design.

Sheet, stone and tiles

There is a wide range of alternatives to carpet and timber flooring, each with its own, unique qualities.

Sheet flooring
Softer and warmer than stone or timber, sheet floorcoverings come in a surprising variety of colours, patterns and textures. They are often available in tile form, too, and can sometimes be cut into graphic patterns.

▶ **Vinyl:** A PVC-based man-made material that is hard-wearing, slip-resistant, quiet and easy to maintain. It tends to be reserved for kitchens and bathrooms, but can be used anywhere you like, and comes in a huge range of textures and patterns, many of them good imitations of stone, wood or ceramic tiles. For a contemporary look, designs include molten metal, sparkling surfaces, abstract prints or photographic images.

▶ **Linoleum:** A traditional material made from renewable sources – linseed oil, tree resin, wood flour, cork powder and pigments from natural ingredients. It offers a wide range of colours and textures, is very durable and naturally anti-bacterial and biodegradable.

▶ **Cork:** Often under-rated, cork is hardwearing, resilient to water and durable. Gone are the orange tones familiar from the 1960s: cork is now available in a range of fashionable shades.

▶ **Rubber:** Both good-looking and practical, rubber is robust, easy to keep clean and tactile, it is available in smooth or textured designs. The latter are ideal for bathrooms. Rubber floors should be laid professionally.

Natural stone
Sandstone, limestone, granite, marble and terrazzo are expensive floorings that have a beautiful, individual grain and patina, and should last a lifetime – but they are also hard, noisy and cold underfoot.

Stone tiles are available in a range of sizes, from mosaics through to large slabs, and a variety of finishes. In areas that might get wet, such as kitchens or bathrooms, choose a version that is matt or slightly textured – sanded for a rough finish, or riven for an attractive, hand-split effect. Avoid marble in the kitchen, though, as it can stain and corrode, and remember that all stone floorings need to be sealed.

Ceramic, porcelain and other tiles

Just like wall tiles, ceramic and porcelain floor tiles are heat- and water-resistant, hardwearing and low maintenance. Thicker than wall tiles, they come in a vast array of shapes, sizes and designs. Unglazed terracotta and quarry tiles are rugged and non-slip but, like any other hard surface, they won't be kind to dropped crockery. Encaustic tiles are a type of patterned ceramic tile very popular in Victorian and Edwardian homes (especially hallways). Distinctive and handsome, they can be restored if they have suffered over the years.

↑ It is always worth trying to restore original flooring like these black and white tiles.

← Period fireplaces often feature original floor tiles but you can create the same effect using tiles of your choice.

↖ Stone flooring with a riven finish is non-slip but can be rough underfoot.

TILES p.96

Lighting

As well as making interiors seem bigger, brighter and fresher, clever lighting can give 'va-va voom' to the simplest of decorative schemes.

When a room seems boring, bland and lifeless, it is often the lighting that is to blame. A well-designed lighting scheme, on the other hand, emphasises good points, highlights colour, texture and shapes, and disguises problem areas. On a practical note, we need adequate lighting to help us carry out day-to-day activities easily and safely. And on a psychological level, light sends out signals of warmth, welcome and vitality – reinforcing a sense of comfort and security.

In many ways, the best lighting is invisible: in other words, you don't notice the fitting itself, just the fact that it illuminates efficiently and beautifully. Ideally, it is best to design a lighting scheme at the earliest stages, when you are planning how a room will be used and where furniture will be placed. Think about how you will live in the space, and then ask yourself where you will need light, how much you will require at different times of day and night, which areas you want to highlight and what effects you wish to create. Only then can you wire in lights or install plug sockets exactly where you'll need them.

There are four main types: overall general light; bright light for working by; accent lighting for special features; and atmosphere lighting, which sets the mood. Try to design a scheme that employs several of these types, using light from more than one direction – think of it as painting with light, creating washes and filling in with highlights and lowlights.

↓ Different periods, but with a similar ethos: curvy metal unites a traditional chandelier and a 1960s-style floor lamp.

Downlights

Either set into the ceiling or mounted onto it, downlights may be fixed or adjustable. A good source of general lighting.

Strip Lights

Functional and often energy saving, these simple lights are useful for working areas such as kitchens or utility rooms.

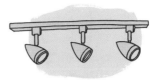

Tracks

A row of spotlights can be attached to a straight or curved track when it is not possible to recess lights in the ceiling.

Spotlight

Individual spotlights are ideal for highlighting special features. In work areas or dark corners, clip-on versions are practical.

Uplighters

Fixed at eye level or higher, uplighters bounce light onto the ceiling and can help make a room seem bigger.

Wall Lights

By diffusing a soft glow around the room, wall lights are an excellent source of general lighting.

Floor Lamps

These tall fittings are useful for adding light to corners of rooms, and perfect next to a reading chair.

Table Lamps

Often inexpensive, table lamps are a versatile way to add light in dark corners and make a room more welcoming.

Shelf Lights

Fitted under a shelf, these lights illuminate the display or work area below. There are also versions for glass shelves.

Desk Lights

A hinged-arm, Anglepoise-style lamp is ideal for illuminating your work. The more adjustable it is, the better.

Pendants

Often hung in the centre of a room, pendant lights range from decorative chandeliers to simple modern fittings.

Outdoor Lights

Security lights, spotlights, floodlights, party lights and decorative solar fittings can transform an outside space.

Lighting room-by-room

Make sure that every room in your home is illuminated beautifully, with bright, clear light for practical tasks, highlights for special features and a warm, welcoming glow for ambience and comfort.

Living rooms
Ideally, install a flexible range of options, from bright reading lights beside seating to softer, ambient lights for relaxing and entertaining. You could also highlight shelving, pictures or a coffee table. Don't forget fires and candlelight, for a romantic, soft glow.

Dining rooms
A pendant hung over a dining table creates an intimate atmosphere (but make sure it is hung above eye level). Fix wall lights a little lower than eye level – it works better when you are sitting down.

Kitchens
Adjustable spotlights, on tracks or in the ceiling, are practical for general light. Mount bright lights (tubes or downlights) beneath wall cabinets to illuminate worksurfaces.

Bathrooms
Combine directional task lights – ceiling downlights or tracks – with softer lights, such as LED wall washers. Because shiny surfaces reflect light, you may need fewer light sources or lower wattages than you expect. Only use fittings designed to be safe in wet and steamy conditions.

Bedrooms
Here subtle, flattering lighting is needed, although a good light for mirrors is essential. Wall-mounted lights free up space on a bedside table.

Halls and stairs
Lighting should be warm and welcoming. Staircases must be brightly and evenly lit, with a switch at the top and bottom.

HOW TO COVER A LAMPSHADE p.27

Quick tricks with lighting

▶ Change the bulb – a brighter or softer one may work better; or try a more mellow tone.

▶ Change the shade – a new shape or colour may make all the difference. But do choose a replacement shade that's in proportion with both the light fitting and the room as a whole.

▶ Use dimmer switches whereever possible and gain complete control over your level of lighting.

▶ Add a lamp in a dark corner: table lamps, floor lamps and even clip-on spotlights can all work wonders.

▶ Extend the cord of a central pendant – you can then change its position by hooking it from a cup hook screwed into the ceiling.

▶ Add fairy lights around mantelpieces or over bedheads for a pretty twinkle.

▶ For extra light outdoors, try solar-powered lanterns or stake lights. They are instant, easy, inexpensive and eco-conscious, too.

▶ Turn your lights right down and light a few candles. They look particularly effective grouped together, and you just can't beat their warm, flickering glow.

← Unusual light fittings can work well even in traditional living rooms.

↖ A wall light facing down provides soft lighting for bedrooms.

→ Concealed blue lighting adds another element of colour in this living room scheme.

Make the most of natural light

▶ Clean the windows.

▶ Remove ornaments from window sills.

▶ Make sure curtains and blinds don't hang in front of windows when open.

▶ Hang a large mirror opposite a window.

▶ Replace a solid door with a glazed one.

▶ Consider enlarging or adding windows, or installing a skylight or sun pipe.

Storage

Good storage can really improve your quality of life: tidying up is quicker and easier, and your home is more spacious and attractive.

↑ Shelves can easily be built into an alcove. A deep 'lip' added to the front makes them appear nicely robust.

↗ Old chests can double up as coffee tables to provide extra storage in small spaces.

HOW TO PUT UP
A SHELF IN AN
ALCOVE p.129

Ten golden rules of storage

1 You can never have too much storage. Aim for it to take up about 10–20 per cent of each room.

2 Plan storage with military precision – it's really worth taking an hour or so to add up what's going to go where and how much space it will require.

3 Don't store items you no longer need. Regularly assess what's vital to your life and, if something's not, sell it, throw it or give it away (See Clear that clutter, below right).

4 If you only need things on rare occasions, store them in attics, basements, sheds or the tops of cupboards. Keep easy-access storage space for the stuff you need all the time.

5 Store small things in small containers and large things in larger containers.

6 Don't place heavy items higher than shoulder height or lower than knee height.

7 Storing things on open shelves is great if you are really tidy and enjoy dusting. If not, fit cupboard doors or use attractive boxes or baskets.

8 Do things keep ending up in the wrong place? Then rethink your storage. A kitchen cupboard might be a better place for toddler toys than a bedroom, for example.

9 Stacking boxes look great and save space – but if you need to get at the contents quickly and easily, don't put them in the bottom boxes.

10 Everyone has an odds and ends drawer (or several), but try not to let yours overflow out of control.

Clear that clutter

▶ Aim to declutter one room per week – or perhaps spend ten minutes decluttering each day. That way it won't be too painful.

▶ Find at least six large bags or boxes, and mark them as follows: 'rubbish', 'recycle', 'give away', 'sell', 'mend' and 'store'. You may also think of other categories that apply to you.

▶ With the bags or boxes near at hand, the sorting becomes simple. And when all you have left is the 'store' container, think carefully about the best place to keep each object. With all that unnecessary clutter out of the way, you will be amazed at how much extra space you can create.

Hallways and living rooms

When thinking about your storage needs, tackle each room individually. Start by making a smart entrance to your home with a well-planned hallway, and creating order in your living room.

A neat and tidy hall

When space is tight, a useful hallway option is a set of shallow, floor-to-ceiling cupboards with plain doors, (painted the same colour as the walls, or mirrored to maximise light) ranked along one wall. For books or an out-of-the-way display, a shelf running the length of the hallway, above head height, works really well. Add a place for post and keys – perhaps a small, wall-mounted cupboard, or a bowl on a shelf and a set of hooks. Don't forget the space beneath the staircase – if you are not already using it as a home office or extra loo, it can be your most essential, multi-purpose cupboard, efficiently equipped with shelves, baskets and hooks.

Organised living

For CDs and DVDs, books and magazines, shelving is vital to keep your living room neat and tidy, and the obvious place to fit it is across the alcoves either side of a chimney-breast. Fit cupboard doors (solid or glazed) in front of the lower shelves for extra versatility. Alternatively, freestanding bookshelves, as tall as possible for maximum storage, can be placed anywhere there is floor and wall space. A chest that doubles up as a coffee table is a handy option and, if you are buying a side table, choose one with slim drawers to accommodate remote controls, letters and such like. Add boxes and baskets if you are still stuck for somewhere to put smaller items.

Fitted or freestanding storage?

Built-in, fitted storage is neater and takes up less room than free-standing pieces. It can cover walls or span alcoves, but is also ideal for awkward spaces such as above doors, under sloping ceilings and beneath bay windows. Think open shelves, cupboards, drawers or whatever suits your needs – designed so as to echo architectural details (such as architraves or door panels) elsewhere in the room. Keep costs down by using pine, chipboard or medium density fibreboard, and finish with primer, undercoat and eggshell paint.

However, free-standing storage can be moved around and is often less expensive than commissioning fitted pieces. Choose a style to suit your interior – anything from an antique Oriental chest to a modern designer sideboard. Found a cheap piece with an ugly veneer? A coat of paint will redeem it. Second-hand finds can be transformed by stripping, painting and changing pulls, knobs or handles. And don't forget smaller storage – boxes and baskets, hooks and hanging rails – to tidy up awkwardly shaped stuff that won't go anywhere else.

← When your storage is glass-fronted, make sure what's inside is kept neat and tidy.

↑ Fitted cupboards in hallways provide neat storage for shoes and coats.

↖ A mix of open shelves and cupboards with doors works well in a living room.

Kitchens and bathrooms

For the most practical, functional rooms in the house, such as kitchens and bathrooms, excellent storage is vital. A combination of tried-and-tested solutions and ingenious ideas will help you keep clutter under control.

← Storage included below sinks helps to conceal messy bathroom clutter and keep surfaces clear.

An orderly kitchen

Get clever in the kitchen and you will find endless options for well-designed storage. In general, try to use the walls as much as possible, going high with full-height cupboards and larders, and utilising unused spaces between wall units and worktops with hanging racks, rails and shelves. Instead of hinged cupboards, base-level drawers in a range of depths allow easier access to contents, while internal divisions help you get better organised. 'Magic corner' cupboards are enormously helpful, and don't forget that shallow storage units can be hung on the back of a broom cupboard or under-stairs door to hold anything from a mop to vacuum cleaner accessories.

Blissful bathrooms

To get the best from your bathroom you need it to be both an oasis for blissful bathing and a functional and efficient space. But it will be neither if you don't get your storage right. The solution is to display only your most attractive accessories, and conceal all the boring or unattractive stuff well out of the way. Make a start with a wall-mounted cupboard or a vanity unit below the basin and add open shelves for folded towels, pretty bottles and the like. Over-the-door hooks and hanging pockets provide masses of storage but take up very little room, as do corner-fitting units, shower shelves with suction pads and storage towers on wheels.

How to put up a shelf in an alcove

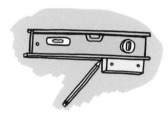

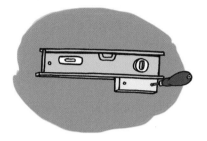

Before you start

Check the walls for wires and pipes using a cable detector. Wear safety goggles and a dust mask when drilling or sawing. For plasterboard walls, you will have to screw your battens to the studs behind the plasterboard.

1 Using a spirit level, draw a pencil line around the inside of the alcove to mark the lower edge of the shelf. Cut lengths of 50 x 25mm (2 x 1in) timber to fit, angling the front ends of the side battens at 45° so they will be less obvious once fitted.

2 Drill pilot holes every 250mm (10in) on the timber batten. Hold the batten against the back wall just below the pencil line and mark where the fixing holes will be. Drill and plug the holes, then attach the batten to the wall using screws that are at least 50mm (2in) long. Repeat for the two side battens.

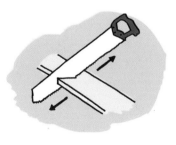

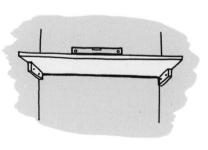

3 Repeat steps 1 and 2 for the remaining shelves in the alcove, then cut the shelves to the correct size – measuring both the front and back of each shelf space accurately for a good fit.

4 If the shelf does not quite fit against the back wall, you may need to scribe it: use a block of wood taped to a pencil to trace the outline of the wall on the shelf, then saw, plane or sand along the line.

5 For extra stability, nail, screw or glue the shelves into position. Prime and paint.

Bedrooms

A bedroom should be a relaxing retreat, which means that well thought-out storage is especially important. The same goes for children's rooms, where smart thinking will help you keep up with their ever-changing requirements.

A calming bedroom

How much bedroom storage do you need? Most people underestimate the amount required, and the only real answer is to take a tape measure and plan it out. Wardrobes fitted wall-to-wall and floor-to-ceiling make the best use of space. Decide whether you need full, half or three-quarter hanging space, and then you will be able to add shelves, drawers, racks or stacking boxes according to how much space you have left. Other options include hanging a shoe rack behind the door, using a small cabinet as a bedside table and employing the large space under the bed for trunks, suitcases or under-bed boxes on wheels.

Keeping kids' kit in check

A combination of open shelves and cupboards is the answer to the incredible mess that can quickly be generated in most children's room. Keep things at child-height, avoid 'themes' that will quickly be outgrown, and screw shelves and wardrobes securely to the wall. In a small room, a raised bed provides great space for both storage and study. To maximise floor area, employ peg rails, hooks, stacking boxes and hanging fabric organisers. Avoid heavy-lidded toy boxes that can trap fingers – coloured plastic buckets are much better. And one last tip: labelling or colour co-ordinating boxes or shelves will make tidying much easier.

← An old locker has been recycled to provide storage in this child's bedroom.

Inspired storage ideas

▶ Think laterally and look for plan chests, lockers, trolleys, hanging racks and other industrial or retail storage at office-supply companies, shop display outlets or second-hand shops. Even old wooden apple crates can make fantastic shelving.

▶ Use wall racks or ceiling pulleys for bikes or similar items.

▶ Create a pegboard wall for storage in a workspace, laundry room, garage or shed.

▶ Add sturdy pockets along the bottom of the curtains in a child's bedroom to store small teddies and other toys.

▶ Tuck cardboard boxes and shoe boxes into cupboards. If they are out on show, cover them with attractive wrapping paper or wallpaper offcuts.

▶ Add a drawstring to an old pillowcase to make a laundry bag for the back of a bedroom or bathroom door.

▶ Use clean jam jars or tin cans to make simple storage pots for pens, brushes or felt tips.

▶ Build storage drawers into the treads of a wooden staircase.

↖ A perfect use for alcoves – built-in wardrobes, with space above for a trunk.

↑ A shelf above the picture rail has been combined with peg rails for hanging clothes.

Technology

Love it or hate it, we can't live without technology.
Make the most of it or hide it away – it's your decision.

↑ Flat screen TVs are much easier to disguise than old-fashioned, deep-backed ones. Mounted on the wall, they can even become part of the artwork.

→ Floating shelves are a great way to store equipment, provided your sockets are close enough to avoid trailing wires.

↓ Adding a shelf in an alcove can create a neat, space-saving media unit.

There is no getting away from the fact that the TV is nearly always the focal point of a modern living room. But it doesn't have to dominate. Avoid purpose-built stands as they are rarely very attractive – you are better off with a side table, low cupboard or shelf that suits the overall style of the room. And it's easy to mount a TV on a swing-arm support or pop it on a wheeled trolley, so you can push it out of sight whenever you wish.

Alternatively, upcycle an old cabinet into an all-purpose media unit (drill holes in the back for leads and to avoid heat build-up) and you can simply shut the doors when the set is off.

Chargers are probably the biggest bugbear of the modern home. For organisation's sake, keep them all in one place – a drawer near a socket is neat and efficient. Or consider buying a single charging station that all your gadgets can sit on. There are all sorts of stands, fasteners, tidies and other inexpensive accessories that are no end of help when it comes to organising techno-jumble; then again, it is possible to do a neat job of it with hand-written labels and wire ties. If your remote control is always getting lost, just stick on some hook-and-loop tape so you can attach it to the side of the TV.

Setting up a home office

▶ List how many things you need to plug in, and work out how many sockets you will need (you'll probably be surprised). Fix several sockets about three inches above your work surface, and have a few hidden lower down, too.

▶ Organise all your electrical items together – so you don't end up with long cables between them.

▶ For a desk in the middle of the room, you will need floor sockets.

▶ Adjustable wall lamps above your working area free up desk space.

▶ Get ergonomic: site your computer monitor straight ahead of you, about an arm's length away; feet should be flat on the floor, with thighs parallel to the floor; your desk should be about elbow height; when typing, your fingers should be lower than your wrists.

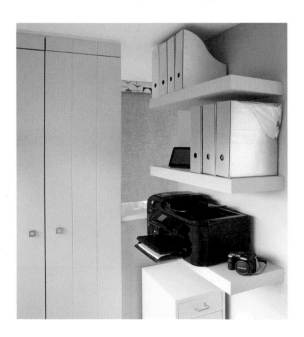

HOW TO PUT UP A SHELF IN AN ALCOVE p.129

Late Victorian Terrace
Salford 1890

In the early 19th century, Salford in the north of England became a hub for the textile industry, boosted by trading links opened up by the railways and Manchester Ship Canal.

Rapid industrialisation created new job opportunities and led to huge population increases, so mill and factory owners built row upon row of terraced houses to accommodate their workforce. But fitting in so many houses meant conditions were often cramped and basic.

The late 19th-century houses shown here were built on what would have been the outskirts of the city – this was the start of commuter life. Living further from the city centre meant that you could have a larger, grander house – reflecting a higher social status.

These properties were built for skilled workers, such as weavers, teachers and engine drivers. A step above the more basic back-to-back housing, these properties had running water and drainage, bay windows and a little front area to show off the relative grandeur of their owners.

▶ Victorian terraced houses often opened straight onto the parlour, with stairs in the middle. These houses feature a narrow hallway, which indicates that they were for the better off.

▶ Originally there would have been two rooms on the ground floor, with the 'front room' for best, used by adults and guests only, and the 'back room' for general living and eating; in these houses the kitchen is situated in a rear extension.

▶ The front room was often the largest in the house; the sizes of other rooms would frequently be sacrificed for larger best rooms. The front room would also be the grandest, with the rest of the house relatively plain.

▶ The dining room would have been the main space where the family relaxed, ate, carried out chores, wrote letters and studied. It would have contained a sideboard, dining table (and chairs), a writing desk in the corner and larger chairs for relaxing.

▶ All these houses featured picture rails. The growing popularity of photographs, prints and art for the home meant that these rails were incredibly practical for hanging decoration without damaging the walls.

▶ Ceiling roses surrounded each light fitting, and had the additional bonus of collecting dust from the hanging gaslights, although they were less popular in this period than in the mid-Victorian era.

▶ Interior design was a dangerous business in the 1890s: white base coat paint contained lead, while various colours of wallpaper (greens, lilacs, blues and greys) contained up to 60 per cent arsenic.

← All the houses were built with iron railings outside; gaps remain where these were taken for the war effort during the Second World War and have not been replaced.

→ The street was built in sections over a number of years. Due to limited funds, speculative builders would purchase a plot at a time, build on it and sell the properties to get enough capital for the next stretch. If you look carefully you can see the raised wall behind the street light.

PERIOD CHARACTER p.9

CASE STUDY | Texture & Interest

A neutral colour palette need not be boring: this room employs different shades, textures and points of interest to great effect.

BRIEF

Jason and Lisa knocked their two reception rooms together about 11 years ago and wanted it to be updated into a modern space for the whole family. They liked neutral and pastel colours and wanted a feature that added interest on either side of the chimney-breast. Storage was a big issue: Jason and Lisa wanted either shelves or closed storage to be incorporated into the design. Some sort of new flooring or floor covering was on their wish list, as well as new lighting and some new furniture, although they were keen to retain their brown leather sofas. Another request was to unify the fireplaces with the same finish, or possibly even to replace them.

BEFORE

↓ The designer's proposal is well-planned, professional and very much in line with the owners' brief.

Layout and design ideas

→ Painted printing blocks make a fun display for the mantelpiece.

▶ The colour scheme has been completely updated using a modern combination of greys.

▶ The original fireplaces have been opened up and renovated.

▶ The family dining area now boasts a bright new table, which complements vintage chairs with newly covered seat pads.

▶ Shelving in the alcoves means that the TV no longer dominates the room, as well as providing useful storage.

▶ The woodwork: skirting, picture rails and doors have all been painted in a darker colour to add definition.

← Woodland wall transfers create an illusion of extra space.

AFTER

↑ Carefully chosen shades of grey and brown create a co-ordinated scheme.

← A pendant light over the dining table adds a touch of period style.

KNOCKING DOWN
WALLS p.89

CASE STUDY | Vibrant Vintage Style

With plenty of wonderful vintage finds to use, this room needed a design scheme that could unite a range of colours, patterns and styles.

BRIEF

Becky and Richard had lived in their house for just under a year. They moved in soon after getting married but had not yet got around to any decorating. They liked shabby chic style and had collected a number of pieces of vintage furniture that needed to be given a new lease of life. They also had a sofa suite that they wanted to keep, along with the oak-effect laminate floor and a dining table and chairs. Becky and Richard were keen to have new lighting, curtains, a rug, radiator covers and storage in which to house their TV and games consoles. They were keen to use colour in moderation, and hoped that the fireplace could be opened up and a fire surround added.

Fun and inspiring

Colour and texture

BEFORE

→ The mood board contains colourful room sketches and inspirational photographs showing decorative ideas.

Sketches and photos

USING PATTERN p.38

▶ A distinctive scheme of pinks, blues and greens complements the owners' existing furniture and love of colour.

▶ The bricked-up fireplace has been opened up and turned into a focal point with the addition of a cast iron fire surround, bought at a reclamation yard.

▶ The dining table and chairs were hand-painted in vivid colours.

▶ Lace curtains and a rag rug nod to the history of the property.

← Family photographs in colourful frames make a fun display.

↓ The bold, bright living space feels contemporary, but with a traditional twist.

AFTER

↑ Built-in
cupboards and
shelves add
useful storage
in the alcove.

DESIGN HIGHLIGHT
↗ The dining table
was given a unique,
hand-painted design
using acrylic eggshell.
A chequer- board effect
emulates the look of an
old-fashioned tablecloth.

CONNECTING
SPACES p.89

← The rag rug is a traditional Victorian feature. Its colours complement those of the sofa.

→ The colour of the ottoman echoes the pretty shade of green on the walls.

CASE STUDY | Spacious & Comfortable

A dramatic change in colour scheme and carefully thought-out decorative effects make this large room feel homely without losing its sense of space.

BRIEF

Kelvin had lived in his Salford terrace for 12 years and was keen for his living room to get a thorough makeover – he last decorated eight years ago. He hoped to retain the existing layout, with the seating area towards the back of the room and the front kept clear. He wanted to keep his teal sofas but hoped that his other mismatching furniture could be incorporated into the decorative scheme. The colour palette he favoured included muted shades of brown, grey, blue and green, and he liked natural textures. Overall he wanted the space to be modern and sophisticated, with a nod to Victorian style.

BEFORE

Design ideas

Neutral backdrop

Sketches

Paint ideas

→ The designer's mood board includes a comprehensive collection of colour swatches, photographic references, as well as sketches of wall effects.

▶ Pale grey walls and white woodwork maximise the feeling of space in the room.

▶ The airy and natural Scandinavian design features period and industrial twists.

▶ Faux book wallpaper makes features of the alcoves, and a hessian-effect wallpaper covers the large chimney breast.

▶ Hand-crafted and natural accessories bring texture to the monochrome scheme.

▶ The painted shelving unit fits neatly in the alcove to one side of the chimney-breast, making use of what had previously been dead space.

↓ Teal sofas provide splashes of colour in this fresh and airy room.

→ A pile of logs adds colour and texture to the fireplace.

AFTER

IDEAS FOR
FEATURE WALLS
p.91

↓ A second-hand desk, upcycled with chalk-based paint, gives the disused alcove a new purpose.

→ Faux-book wallpaper furnishes the room without needing to add other decorative accessories. It also reflects light.

↓ The chimney breast is covered with hessian-effect wallpaper to add texture without dominating the room.

FITTING IN A HOME OFFICE p.85

Project

The designers at the Salford terrace were each given a painted wooden clock to personalise and incorporate into their design. Why not use a stencil to add your individual stamp to a simple wooden object?

Victorian-style painted wood effect.

Old maps and copper gilding.

Comic-book découpage.

HOW TO ADD A STENCIL TO A WOODEN OBJECT

1 First make sure your wooden object is dry and clean from dust. Choose a stencil – there are a wide range available to buy or you could even make your own. Tape the stencil into place using masking tape and ensure that all areas you do not want to be painted are properly covered.

2 The best way to get an even finish is to use aerosol paint. Spray through the stencil with light even coats to build up coverage gradually, making sure you spray straight down so that the spray does not get under the stencil. Wait about 30 minutes before removing the stencil and then allow to dry for 8–12 hours.

3 Once dry, apply a clear varnish with a brush or you can use a spray.

The history of the kitchen

More money is spent on the kitchen than any other room in the house – but it was once a humble space that was home to backbreaking drudgery.

The kitchen as we know it is a relatively recent innovation. Not much more than 100 years ago or so, it was the norm for servants to cook on a coal-fired, cast-iron range, without the benefits of either refrigeration or hot running water, in a poorly ventilated basement separated, as far as possible, away from the rest of the household.

Go back even further, and the earliest 'kitchen' was a rudimentary affair – for the medieval peasant, at least, who had nothing more than an open fire in the middle of his one-room hut. At the other end of the scale, the kitchens of grand houses and palaces boasted an inconceivable number of different areas for storing and preparing food, and even had brick chimneys to keep the rooms free of smoke.

But kitchens were a fire risk, and the smell of cooking was considered socially unacceptable – so the middle and upper classes kept their kitchens well away from living, sleeping and dining areas, sometimes even erecting separate buildings to house them.

As technology developed, the cast-iron range was introduced, along with hundreds of kitchen tools and appliances, from basic food processors to early freezers but, for all but the poorest who still ate, slept and cooked in the same room, the kitchen was never part of the genteel home.

Everything changed after the First World War. Not only had the Upstairs, Downstairs model of household management all but disappeared, but the introduction of gas and electricity supplies to most households in Britain by the 1930s meant that all sorts of labour-saving devices were available to the housewife who suddenly found she had to manage without hordes of staff. It was time to reinvent the kitchen for the modern age.

The 'Frankfurt kitchen' of 1926, designed to be space-saving and inexpensive, was a forerunner of the modern fitted kitchen. However, things really took off after the Second World War, when Britain embraced the American 'dream kitchen', a place in which doing the cooking, washing up, washing of clothes and ironing was not domestic drudgery but supposedly enjoyable, thanks to ranks of colourful, fitted cupboards with wipe-clean tops and, of course, gadgets galore. The modern kitchen had, at last, arrived.

The final stage in the kitchen evolution came when the aspirational middle classes began to renovate their period homes, knocking down walls and introducing the concept of open-plan living. The kitchen, be it Victorian country style or high-tech haven, became an integral part of our social space, no longer hidden from view but now an area in which to relax, entertain and demonstrate both interior design skills and culinary prowess – all in the new heart of the home.

Kitchens

What makes a good-looking, functional kitchen – where you can cook, eat and spend time together as a family? Careful planning is the answer.

First, assess exactly what you need from the kitchen. Ask yourself lots of questions. Who will use it and how often? How will it be used – for regular family meals or the occasional microwave dinner? And what about other activities – homework, watching TV, doing the washing or ironing? Do you have lots of kitchen gadgets and will you keep them on worktops or in cupboards? Do you prefer solid or glass-fronted cupboards, or lots of open shelves? Will you have some unfitted elements, such as a dresser or sideboard? Would you prefer built-in or freestanding appliances? What about worktops, sinks and flooring? Next, do plenty of research, and visit every showroom within reach. Consider what styles you like, and what you can afford. Ultimately, it's best to avoid fashion fads, invest in quality and, above all, go with what feels right for you.

How to plan a kitchen

Deciding where the sink will go is often a good place to start when designing a kitchen. From there, it is usually best to place the main food preparation area between the sink and the hob, ensuring that this worktop space is large enough to serve up a meal, and has enough power points nearby for small appliances. Depending on your hob/cooker, it may need to go against an exterior wall or chimney, and it should certainly be sited so that hot pans can be carried to the sink easily. Place the fridge at the end of a run of cupboards. Remember to allow enough space around your appliances to open doors comfortably. Experts recommend a 'work triangle' between the cooker, sink and fridge. This may not work for you but aim to leave an uninterrupted space between the areas you use the most.

Kitchen layouts

Single line

The only option if your kitchen is along one wall. Place the sink between the fridge and hob, and try to maximise the length of work surface, fitting built-in appliances below and wall units above.

Galley

In a narrow kitchen you can fit a line of units and appliances along each side. When well designed, this can be extremely convenient, though it is best for a one- or two-person home.

U-shaped

A U-shape gives plenty of storage and working space, but only possible if you have stretches of wall on three sides. In a large room, be wary of having to walk too far from one side to the other.

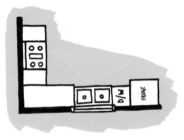

L-shaped

This layout is useful in a square or rectangular kitchen if you need space for a table, and if two people are using the kitchen at the same time. Plan the corner carefully to avoid a clash of doors.

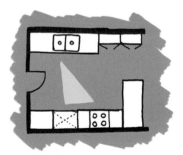

Peninsula

Add a unit at right angles to one end of a U- or L-shaped kitchen, and you have a peninsula. Very handy as a breakfast bar or extra work surface that can be accessed from both sides.

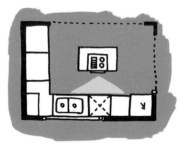

Island

An island gives extra storage and workspace as well as an eating area. Don't make it so big you can't reach the middle and plan the room so that you are not constantly walking round it.

Kitchen cupboards

From the most traditional, solid-wood, Shaker-style kitchen unit to the glossiest of flat-fronted, lacquered modern versions, there really are endless styles of kitchen cupboard to choose from.

↑ In small kitchen and dining areas making the most of your space is a must; white cupboards will stop the room feeling dark.

→ Open shelves above a run of cupboards work well in most kitchens.

Colour, finish and style are not your only worktop choices. Do you want units that are machine-made or individually constructed by hand? Budget will probably help you decide, and it's worth bearing in mind that machine-made units are not necessarily poor quality, though they will have 'plant-on' doors that sit in front of the frame, rather than 'in-frame' doors, which have to be individually made.

If you want to avoid the bland, box-like look of the conventional fitted kitchen, vary things by specifying wall cupboards of different heights or colours, or replacing some solid cupboard doors with glass fronts. For a more open look, opt for base units on legs rather than those hidden by plinths, replace wall units with shelves, hooks and racks, and create interesting displays of your crockery, glassware and most attractively packaged food.

Fitting your kitchen

When buying a fitted kitchen, ensure that you are clear on who will install it – does the company have a team of experienced fitters, or will you have to find someone yourself? If you are buying a flatpack, are you confident in your own abilities to put it together? Just remember: a good fitter can make an average kitchen look amazing, while poor fitting can make even an expensive kitchen look terrible.

Unfitted kitchens

Fitted kitchens are the norm these days, but you can still add one or two free-standing pieces to create a charming, informal look – or even create an entire kitchen from assorted cupboards, tables, dressers and shelves. The trick to mixing and matching is to plan in advance, ensuring that adjacent pieces are very similar in depth and height, that wall units and shelves are aligned in order to create visual coherence, and that you have a pleasing blend of materials, colours and finishes.

Update your kitchen cupboards

1 Remove the doors and drawer fronts and take off the handles, hinges and any other hardware.

2 Thoroughly sand everything you plan to paint or stain.

3 Mask the areas on the insides of the carcasses that you don't want to paint.

4 Carefully apply a suitable primer, undercoat and topcoat, or a wood stain.

5 Replace any hinges that are worn or not working properly and, if necessary, change the knobs or handles, too (you may need to fill holes if they don't match the existing ones).

Worktops

Worktops and splashbacks can dramatically alter the character of a kitchen. As well as looking good, they must be tough and durable, too.

First things first, worktops must be easy to clean, without nooks and crannies that can harbour germs. They must be tough enough to withstand wear and tear, and resistant to knives, heat, steam and water. Splashbacks and upstands (their smaller cousins) should be smooth, wipeable, waterproof and durable enough to protect the walls behind your sink and hob. Because every material has its own, unique qualities, your best option may be to fit different surfaces in different areas of your kitchen.

Having considered the practicalities, next comes the fun part. There are endless choices of material, colour and finish for both worktops and splashbacks.

Most materials can be used for both surfaces (usually cut thinner when used vertically), so you can opt for a seamless, all-over look, or mix and match for an interesting effect. You can choose a surface that will blend into the background, or create a look-at-me, wow-factor feature. You may prefer natural colours or dramatic, vibrant shades. One thing is sure: whatever your style, there's a surface to suit you.

↑ Wooden worktops have a classic look but need to be sealed regularly to keep them in good condition.

Types of worktop

Stone

Granite is the toughest option. Slate, limestone and marble are more porous and need treating with a specialist sealant.

Stone composites

Made using a mixture of crushed quartz and a bonding agent, composites are strong and non-porous.

Timber

An elegant, warm and timeless option, but it does need regular sealing. End-grain hardwood makes a good inset cutting area.

Bamboo

With a distinctive grain, bamboo is hard-wearing. It can be sanded just like timber, but needs regular maintenance.

  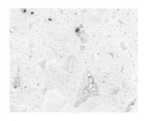 

Concrete

This comes in a range of colours and finishes. Heat- and stain-resistant, hard-wearing and waterproof when sealed.

Laminates

Usually less expensive than timber and available in many colours and patterns, some of which mimic natural surfaces.

Manmade solid surfaces

These are made from a mix of acrylic resin and minerals. Stain-resistant, non-porous, easy to clean and durable.

Metal

Stainless steel is hygienic, heatproof, waterproof and hard-wearing. Thick steel is recommended for durability.

 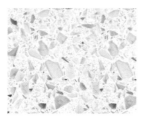

Glass

Glass surfaces come in a range of colours, and are heat-resistant, easy to clean and totally waterproof. Scratches are a risk.

Recycled materials

Options include recycled glass, plastic and industrial and consumer waste.

Sinks, taps and hoods

A good-looking sink fitted with beautiful taps is often the focal point of a kitchen. And don't forget the cooker hood – as well as a practical necessity, it can be a decorative enhancement to your scheme.

Selecting a sink

Kitchen sinks come in all sorts of shapes, sizes, colours and materials – your ideal choice is a sink that has the ability to withstand hard usage as well as good looks that complement your other fixtures, materials and general colour scheme.

Choose from stainless steel, ceramic, composite stone or even timber, copper or concrete. Sinks can be undermounted, inset, farmhouse-style or even moulded from the same material as the worktop. As for size, you may opt for a compact or corner sink to suit a tiny space, a one-and-a-half bowl version

with a drainer that means you can wash up and rinse at the same time, or an oversized sink to cope with large pans and utensils.

Types of taps

Choose a tap that suits the style and size of your kitchen and works with your water pressure. Check that it is high enough to get your pans under, and reaches properly over the sink. For best quality, look for a solid metal body with ceramic discs in the cartridge. A handy option is a pull-out spray tap that lets you rinse your washing up quickly and easily.

▶ **Pillar:** This has two taps, one hot, one cold, with cross-head or lever handles.

▶ **Monobloc:** One tap mixes hot and cold water, controlled via one or two handles or levers.

▶ **Wall-mounted:** A tap that frees up space and makes cleaning easier.

▶ **Pull-out:** Features an extendable spray hose.

▶ **Swivel:** An essential tap for reaching both bowls of a double sink.

▶ **Water filter:** Add a water filter to reduce impurities in your water

▶ **Boiling water:** This tap provides boiling water instantly (there are safety features built in).

▶ **Colour-changing:** An LED light ring illuminates the water.

Cooker hoods

A cooker hood is essential to get rid of steam and smells. There are two types: those which extract, via ducting, to the outside of your house, and those that filter out odours and smoke, then recirculate the clean air back into your kitchen. Before you buy, you'll need to know the extraction rate – ideally 12 times an hour – and check how noisy the extractor is when it's switched on. There are all sorts of style options, from totally concealed, integrated hoods to statement-making versions that double up as stunning light fittings.

← A matt black monobloc tap contrasts well with a chrome sink.

→ This stainless steel cooker hood gives a modern touch.

Arts and Crafts
Moseley 1890

In the 19th century six million homes were built, making it the biggest housing boom Britain had seen. It was a period when architects and developers were experimenting with design, and many revivalist styles were apparent: black and white timber façades – called magpie work – were reminiscent of Tudor half-timbered houses, while Baroque white plasterwork imitated 17th-century Queen Anne designs. Another important influence at the time was the Arts and Crafts style.

Started in the 1850s as a reaction against mass production, the Arts and Crafts movement harked back to a romanticised past when craftsman were celebrated for their artistry. Arts and Crafts architecture was formal but individual, it had substance, but wasn't overly elaborate; sentiments that perfectly matched the aspirations of middle class Victorians. The style became immensely popular, and has influenced British architecture ever since.

One of leading proponents of the Arts and Crafts movement was the poet, socialist and art critic, John Ruskin. The prevailing style of the mid-1800s was Neo-classical, a geometrically rigid style that had become established in the Georgian era. Ruskin rejected this 'haughty aristocratic style' as a European import that had little to do with the traditions of British craftsmanship.

Ruskin wanted designers to be at the forefront of many walks of life, including architecture, to help create a more attractive world that reflected the golden age of Victorianism. The altruistic principles of the Arts and Crafts movement made it popular, but there was a fundamental problem with creating hand crafted, lovingly designed objects. It took time and effort, and was ultimately so expensive so that it could only ever be afforded by the rich.

▶ Arts and Crafts houses revelled in their uneven façades and irregular roof heights.

▶ The Arts and Crafts influence is visible in the gable roof with end pegs – showing off the craft of the construction is a hallmark of the Arts and Crafts style, as are the hanging terracotta tiles. Terracotta was perfect for Birmingham as the city had no local stone and the material was resistant to soot and smoke.

▶ In the 1890s builders realised the snob value of doors and added graining, stucco panels, columns, and following encouragement from the Post Office in the middle of the century, the Victorians finally began to adopt the letterbox.

▶ The stained glass window was also the perfect opportunity for designers to show their skill; it harked back to the ornate stained glass of revival and gothic churches. But, by this stage, the increasingly ornate and elaborate designs had little to do with piety, and more to do with showing off.

← The timber work on this house reflects the influence of the Tudor style of the 16th century, as does the tall, sculpted brick chimney.

→ The use of hanging terracotta tiles was a popular gable style on speculative Arts and Crafts houses.

▶ The Victorian era was one of domestication and privacy – the moment at which a man's home became his castle, and his public affairs became completely isolated from his personal life. In this way the Victorians invented what we now think of as the family home.

▶ The design of the early Victorian household was highly specialised, with rooms added for single occasions: morning rooms, front parlours, billiard rooms, libraries, studies, dining rooms – all variations on a theme of purpose. But by the 1890s, people started to reject the idea that having more, smaller rooms was better than fewer, larger rooms, perhaps beginning the trend for the increasingly open-plan style of today.

▶ Hallways, that had been merely a passageway for most of the Victorian era, started to grow again, with the 'hall parlour' a room of its own, featuring a small fireplace and maybe a chair or two. It was the only place that young couples were permitted to spend time together.

▶ Fireplaces in Arts and Crafts houses were incredibly grand; true Arts and Crafts fireplaces were reminiscent of inglenooks, and would have filled the room.

▶ The Victorian love of knick-knacks came from the fact that the world was a precarious place, and a barricade of possessions was used to reinforce a household's position.

▶ The sheer amount of things in an 1890s drawing room meant that they took hours to clean, and even then people were concerned about the dust, soot and grime that accumulated.

The history of the bathroom

The bathroom didn't even exist as a separate room 150 years ago – it has evolved from a communal experience to a private sanctuary of cleanliness and relaxation.

The Romans may have been famous for their sophisticated baths, but in Britain bathing has had a mixed history. Returning Crusaders first introduced Middle Eastern-style communal bathhouses to Britain in the 12th century, in which customers 'stewed' themselves in hot water and could also enjoy a haircut and a hot meal. But the 'stews' were closed by Henry VIII during the 16th century when they degenerated into little more than brothels, and in Tudor times washing habits were limited, to say the least. Meanwhile, going

to the loo meant communal privies for the poorest, chamber pots for the better off (the contents frequently tossed into the street) and padded chairs containing a pot (emptied by a servant) for the wealthy.

Britain's first flushing toilet was invented in 1596, but the idea didn't catch on for another couple of centuries; advances were made in other areas, however, and in Georgian times some households were lucky enough to have a plumbed water supply – though ablutions still mostly consisted of a jug, bowl and washstand in the corner of the bedroom. It didn't help that in 1712 soap was taxed so heavily that it became a luxury item.

All this was to change with the Industrial Revolution from the mid-18th century onwards – and the development of a flushing loo with 'S' and 'U' bends to trap smells. After the 'Great Stink' of 1858, London benefited from the world's first purpose-built sewage system, which spread to the rest of the country at the same time as manufacturers competed to produce an affordable, modern toilet. Within a few years, indoor plumbing became widely available, and it reached a new room in the house – the separate bathroom.

For the poorest Victorians, bathing was still communal, while the aristocracy maintained the tradition of servants carrying water to freestanding baths in bedrooms. But for the burgeoning middle classes, regular bathing became de rigeur and when, in the early 20th century, the high pressure boiler was invented, there was no stopping the development of the bathroom as we now know it, with hot and cold water on demand. From about the 1930s onwards, new homes were built with a separate, indoor bathroom as standard, and gradually the older housing stock was converted – even though in 1951 a third of Britain's households still did not possess a plumbed-in bath. How rapidly times have changed.

From the indoor bathroom it was but a small step to the whirlpool bath, the avocado suite and the rainwater shower. Whereas once hundreds of people shared the same bathing and toilet facilities, today we expect ensuites and as many bathrooms as there are bedrooms. In just a few decades, the newest room in our homes has become a private and personal space dedicated to technology, relaxation and luxury.

Bathrooms

Combine the practical and the indulgent to create a bathroom haven that's as luxurious as it is good-looking

When planning a bathroom, ask yourself who will use it and how often, as well as how much space is available. Have you got room for a bath and a walk-in shower? Do you want a bidet, a pair of basins (handy if there are two of you getting ready for work at the same time), a built-in linen cupboard or a heated towel rail? Will space-saving fittings make a difference? It is always a good idea to plan everything carefully on graph paper, noting the positions of pipes, windows and doors, and allowing generous activity space for knees, elbows, drying and so on around each fitting. If possible, it is visually neater to run pipes under floors and behind slim false walls. And it's not wasted space – punch shallow shelves and cupboards into the false walls and you can create fabulously useful fitted storage.

Keep it simple

Bathroom fittings are available in a multitude of styles and prices, but simplicity is often the best way forward: plain, inexpensive designs can look wonderful when teamed with interesting accessories, and a sensible option is to invest more in moving parts, such as shower doors and taps. How a bathroom feels is vital, in terms of textures and temperatures against bare skin, and underfloor heating gives an efficient, overall heat, while freeing up space against the walls – perhaps for a statement towel warmer. And lighting is important in creating an efficient atmosphere for a quick morning shower, or a more relaxing ambience for an evening bath.

DESIGNING A ROOM LAYOUT p.87

↖ Careful planning will ensure that your new bathroom meets all your needs.

↑ Iridescent mosaic tiles add sparkle to this wet room design.

Quick ways to revamp your tiles

1 If you don't like the colour or pattern of your tiles, paint over them. First, sand the tiles to scuff the surface and then clean both the tiles and the grout scrupulously with sugar soap. Apply tile paint with either a natural bristle brush or a gloss roller. If the colour change is dramatic, you may need a second coat. Leave to dry, then redraw the grout lines with a special pen.

2 Give plain tiles a makeover with stickers – they come in a number of different designs, and are durable, wipeable and, if you change your mind, you can just take them off. They are relatively easy to apply (the surface must be smooth and clean), provided you mark their positions carefully.

3 To rejuvenate discoloured grout, either use a grout pen or, if your grout is beyond repair, remove it with a grout rake, clean up and apply fresh grout. It will look as good as new. You can also freshen up old sealant by scraping it out carefully with a knife blade and reapplying using a mould-resistant type.

Fixtures and fittings

Your choice of bathroom fittings will determine the look of the whole room. There is a wealth of styles to choose from, but make sure they also suit your needs and your budget.

When choosing baths, showers, basins and loos, cast your inhibitions aside. In the showroom, stand in the shower, climb into the bath and sit on the loo. It's the only way to tell whether they are comfortable and feel well made. And ask your retailer how products have been tested, whether they confirm to British or European standards and what guarantee is on offer.

Baths: The more you pay for a bath, the more variety there is in size, shape and material. A standard bath is a 1,700 x 700mm (67 x 27½in) rectangle, but you can also find double-ended and freestanding baths, and a variety of shapes. Acrylic is most common but, if money were no object, you could choose a bath made from stone, wood, copper or glass.

Showers: Look for three key features: flow control, thermostatic control and easy cleaning. The more you pay, the more features you get, including

accurate constant temperature control, a hot water safety limiter, cool housing, water-saving, adjustable sprays and easy-clean functions.

Basins: The traditional option is a pedestal style in ceramic, but there are lots of other styles, including winged, semi-pedestal, counter-top or wall-hung. You can tell a good quality basin by its weight and clean, straight lines.

WCs: Basic loos are of the pan and cistern variety, but if you pay a little more you could go for a close-coupled style (the pan and cistern are in one seamless unit), a back-to-wall WC where the cistern is hidden behind either a false wall or furniture, or a swish, wall-hung type.

↑ Wall-hung sinks and a contemporary freestanding bath.

Wet rooms

If you enjoy an indulgent shower then a wet room is an interesting option – it's simply a waterproof, walk-in shower area (pretty much any shape or size you like), with a drain in the floor, a drenching showerhead and (sometimes) a glass screen. Spacious and stylish, wet rooms are often seen as the last word in luxury, but there are pitfalls. Wet room walls and floors must be made completely watertight by covering with sheeting or sealant. You will also need a suitable drainage slope (or a pre-formed tray), high water pressure and – to prevent condensation and mould – tip top ventilation.

Time to relax

▶ **Hydro-massage baths:** Designed to reduce stress, relax and rejuvenate, hydro-massage baths bubble away your aches and pains just like a masseur's fingers. They can also improve circulation and skin tone, and help you sleep. There are two distinct types of operation: whirlpool baths, which usually have half a dozen or so strong jets of water directed at specific areas, and spa baths, featuring hundreds of tiny holes in the base of the bath which bubble air upwards for a softer, fizzy feeling over the whole body.

▶ **Chromatherapy:** For the last word in relaxation, try chromatherapy in the bath or shower. A sequence of coloured lights washes through the water or steam, and can be paused, if you wish, to complement your mood. It's said that reds, oranges and yellows boost circulation and stimulate the senses, while blues, greens and pinks relax the mind and body.

↗ Whirlpool baths give you a spa-like experience in your own home.

▶ **Aromatherapy:** Some baths and showers offer built-in aromatherapy, where essential oils are diffused as a gentle, scented mist to aid physiological and mental wellbeing. Lavender, for example, is a staple for relaxation and sleep-inducement, while grapefruit boosts energy and eucalyptus clears the mind.

▶ **Super showers:** Shower poles (or towers) combine several body sprays, ranging from a fine mist to a powerful drench, the former sometimes mixing air with water for a rain-like effect, the latter perhaps coming from a 'blade' showerhead. If you want to get gadgety, digital programming means that you can control the various elements of your shower from a single interface, with pre-programmed massage and temperature therapies for a truly spa-like experience. For an even more multi-functional shower, just add steam. Basic requirements are vapour-tight doors, a steam generator and a seat, but to that can be added foot massage, hands-free telephone, MP3 connection and waterproof TV.

Finishing touches

With some thoughtful finishing touches and a few gorgeous accessories, even the most basic of bathrooms can be transformed into a stylish sanctuary.

Tip-top taps
Change the taps (a quick and easy job for any plumber) and an old basin will take on a whole new look. In the same vein, it's also easy enough to replace the handset on many showers.

Sitting pretty
Put a new seat on your loo. A simple white style will freshen up the overall look, while a wooden one has a natural, homely effect. Or you could opt for a funky, modern seat featuring bold colours and patterns – anything from a Union Jack to fish, glitter or barbed wire.

Shower power
Swap a mouldy old shower curtain for a fresh new one – or even replace it with a glamorous glass screen.

Tile style
Changing small areas of tiling need not be too arduous – eye-catching mosaic is ideal, or else a sleek glass panel in a dramatic colour.

Mirror, mirror
A new mirror is great for increasing the sense of light and space, and vital for all sorts of bathroom activities. It can also become a decorative feature in its own right.

Treat your windows
A new window treatment makes a world of difference. Blinds are cost-effective and can be co-ordinated with your overall scheme, while window film is fun, inexpensive and easy to apply.

← Metallic mosaic tiles and
a stunning mixer tap.

↓ → Built-in or freestanding
cupboards help to keep
bathroom surfaces clear.

Sort your storage
Co-ordinate all your small storage items, from wicker
baskets to crackle-glazed pots or bright plastic tubs;
it's all about setting the scene with colour, pattern
and texture.

Art on the wall
Add beautifully framed paintings or photographs
(though perhaps not in very humid areas) to add
character and interest.

Hotel-style luxury
Buy a new set of co-ordinating towels – the larger
and fluffier the better. It's an inexpensive change that
will make you feel like a star.

A bathroom
on a budget

▶   No-frills white bathroom fittings are much
cheaper than designer ones – use tiles, taps and
accessories to create an elegant and upmarket
effect. But remember that not all whites are quite
the same shade. It can be tricky to match them if
you are buying from a variety of online retailers.

▶   Plan your new bathroom carefully so as
to avoid moving existing plumbing – and keep
installation costs down.

▶   A radiator that doubles up as a towel rail will
save you buying the two items separately.

▶   Save on tiling by going only to half-height
around the room, or else just do the splashbacks next
to the bath and basin. Use paint everywhere else.

**BLISSFUL
BATHROOMS p.128**

Edwardian Townhouses
Muswell Hill 1900–07

It wasn't until the turn of the 20th century that Muswell Hill in north London changed from a rural suburb to a popular residential area. In 1896 local developer James Edmondson purchased two large estates giving him 12ha (30 acres) in the heart of the village. He created shopping parades and two wide avenues. Over the next ten years, Edmondson and other developers acquired more land and constructed generously proportioned, well built houses that attracted middle-class residents to the area.

By the time the houses seen here were built, Muswell Hill was already popular with clerks and accountants who worked in the city and commuted to their suburban homes in the evening. It still contains many sturdy examples of Edwardian architecture.

The majority of houses built in this period were solid red brick structures with slate or clay roof tiles, ornate details in plaster or stone (called pargetting) and white-painted wood. Subtle differences, such as terracotta tiles on the gables, elaborate woodwork on the porches and the styles of the windows – all added a degree of variation to this basic structure.

Although they appear to be semi-detached, these houses are actually terraced. Together with their size and layout, each pair is slightly different to the rest, giving an impression of a detached style while maintaining the density and shared walls of terraced properties. On many similar streets, the connecting walls would have been set back even further, with doorways for staff and tradesmen on the side wall – the 'tradesman's entrance'.

▶ The hallways were wide and very grand – a good way for Edwardians to show off their status. The staircases featured a slight twist, another status symbol, as the Edwardians favoured twisting designs and elaborately carved banisters.

▶ Edwardian interior style was a breath of fresh air after the clutter and dark colours of Victoriana, although it would still have seemed crowded by today's minimalist standards.

▶ The curtains in these rooms would have been plain or floral, to co-ordinate with the walls. Roller blinds were also becoming popular for those who saw the downside of dust-collecting curtains.

▶ Edwardian bedroom wallpaper was often 'candy striped', alternating a bright colour with white in thick stripes. Wallpaper also reflected the new style of Art Nouveau, and long, flowing forms and elegant floral patterns were popular.

← The houses as they looked in 1912; the elaborate pargetting in the gable end is plain here – they were painted white at a later date.

→ The line of front gardens creates a boundary wall between house and pavement and adds to the sense of privacy. The front gate, tiled pathway and wooden porch increase the feeling of the 'home as your castle'.

PERIOD
CHARACTER p.9

▶ The Edwardian house would have been a mix of different styles both inside and out. At this time there was a fashion for reproduction furniture (the wing-back chair was particularly popular) and so no one style would have dominated. In many households this would have been a financial issue, as few could afford the expense of a house and all its furnishings, but in these grand town houses the eclectic style would have been equally fashionable.

▶ The feeling of light would have continued in the bedrooms. If the Edwardians still took themselves rather seriously in their reception rooms, their bedrooms allowed more scope for a light touch.

▶ The wooden floors would have been highly polished or stained, with large rugs laid over the top: this was the time for large, rich Dagestan rugs, often mimicked by Persian or Turkish equivalents.

▶ The iron fireplaces featured magnificent surrounds that acted as a frame for Art Nouveau tiles with scrolling floral designs.

CASE STUDY Dramatic Pattern

It can be difficult to make large bedrooms feel furnished. The solution here was to use colour and pattern lavishly to create a truly sumptuous room.

BRIEF

Deborah and John share their house with their two children. They had last decorated their master bedroom 12 years ago, and felt the room was bland, boring and dated. They were hoping for a fresh, modern look that would work with the Edwardian style of the property. The couple loved their bed but had decided that everything else could be replaced, including furniture, lighting, flooring and window treatments. They were also in dire need of a proper wardrobe. The couple wanted to have a vibrant and modern wall covering or paint colour on one or two walls, with a muted shade on the rest, but were keen to avoid dark, sludgy colours.

BEFORE

↓ The designer's proposal is rich in pattern and colour and includes a floor plan.

Wallpaper ideas

→ The scroll pattern on the side table echoes the style of the bed.

▶ The colour scheme is contemporary, with grey walls and modern, graphic wallpaper set within a giant 'frame' made from Edwardian-style architrave.

▶ A new grey wool carpet is warm and soft underfoot and disguises the orangey pine floorboards.

▶ A simple box pelmet conceals the track for the full-length, patterned curtains, which were made using bargain fabric from remnants.

▶ A tall fitted wardrobe solves their storage problems, and the owners' traditional chest of drawers were updated with a coat of white paint.

▶ Old and new mix wonderfully: the mock Rococo French bed is a great contrast to the bold wall behind.

▶ The original pendant light was in keeping with the room as a whole, so was retained.

AFTER

↓ The chest of drawers has been painted to match the scheme.

← A quilted bed cover in the owners' favourite cerise pink is luxurious and inviting.

PATTERN
p.36

CASE STUDY
A Cool, Calm Oasis

Already a peaceful haven, this room benefitted from a fresh eye and some interesting new features.

BRIEF

Clare had lived in her house for 26 years and hadn't touched the decor in the master bedroom since she decorated when she first moved in. She loved the room but felt it was time to remove furniture and update the decor to create an oasis of liveable calm. The Art Nouveau tiles in the fireplace had previously been a source of inspiration, and Clare still wanted the colour scheme to be based around them, in hues of grey, blue, cream or yellow. She asked for new ceiling and bedside lighting, new carpets or flooring, and possibly an upholstered headboard. She also had some furniture she liked but was keen to see updated.

BEFORE

Careful planning

Design details

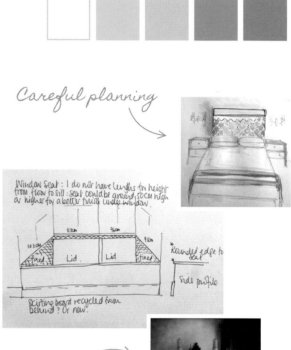

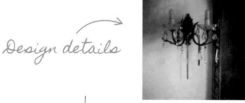

→ The designer's mood board features detailed sketches of proposals. It includes dimensions and showed how new elements would work, which was helpful for the client.

→ The seat for the dressing table was also reupholstered in richly-patterned fabric.

▶ Warm, gentle grey walls and wardrobes look good with the owners' dark furniture. They also highlight the pretty fireplace.

▶ One wall, and the antique linen bed cover, were hand-rollered to create a ghost-like pattern.

▶ Found in a skip, the painted bedside table is now a perfect Edwardian-style piece of furniture.

▶ Repositioning the bed (now with a gently distressed headboard and new wall lights above) makes for a better layout in the room overall, which also has a work zone in one corner.

↓ The serene scheme of muted greys includes a subtle, wallpaper-like pattern on one wall.

AFTER

A GOOD NIGHT'S SLEEP p.183

↑ The grey scheme shows off the colour of Clare's dark furniture, at the same time making it feel more modern.

DESIGN HIGHLIGHT
A window seat, with softly pretty Roman blinds above, creates a serene place to sit. Cushions co-ordinate with the recovered family heirloom chair.

UPHOLSTERY
p.200

↑ Roman blinds are always elegant and help large windows to look dressed without making the room feel dark.

↓ A clever shelf above the door provides space for storage and display.

← Cushions and upholstery do not need to match for a room to look good.

JUDGE'S VIEW

'Getting rid of the curtains and putting in Roman blinds in a ticking stripe has updated the bay window. It gives a soft, casual air to the room. It's a shame there was not enough time to make the upholstered window seat.'

Elegant & Relaxing

Alison wanted her bedroom to be a peaceful sanctuary where she could enjoy time for herself – but first she had to lose an enormous wardrobe.

BRIEF

Alison, her husband Paul and their two children had been living in their house for a year. Although they had renovated the lower part of the house, they hadn't yet tackled the master bedroom. The room was flooded with daylight through the huge period windows, and was a great size, but was dominated by a huge, dark wardrobe. Alison was keen for the room to have a light, calm and modern feel while being sympathetic to the Edwardian period. She was not keen on shabby chic. In terms of colours, she favoured duck egg blue, white, cream, grey and taupe; fabrics included linen, cotton, silk and velvet. Alison also wanted a window seat, and for the floor to be given a lighter finish.

Muted colours

Sketches and photos

BEFORE

→ Colour swatches, photographs and sketches of design ideas all feature on the mood board.

Vintage inspiration

JUDGE'S VIEW
The fireplace is a triumph – it was made from nothing. But I'd have painted the inside a darker colour and maybe had a few candles in it.'

▶ Removing the wardrobes allowed more versatility with the room's layout – the bed was repositioned to create a more spacious feel.

▶ Metallic, damask-style wallpaper sets the tone for the rest of the room. The other walls and the furniture were painted in muted taupes.

▶ The designer used the wood from the wardrobe to make a new fire surround, and painted the brickwork to match the walls.

▶ A trompe l'oeil headboard made from MDF was painted with chalk paint – a quirky nod towards an iron headboard.

←↓ Rustic and hand-made accessories, including salvaged laundry tubs as bedside tables, add a personal touch.

AFTER

DESIGN HIGHLIGHT

↓ The mirror frame is painted to co-ordinate with the room, with a touch of gilding showing through in a vintage style.

↓ Découpaged letters were made from torn-up sheet music that was bought at a car boot sale.

→ These simple, mismatching frames complement the rustic, softly coloured scheme.

↑ A painted MDF front attached to a low shelf has become a trompe l'oeil desk.

JUDGE'S VIEW

The room is beautifully styled and has a nice feel about it. The colour really works. It's great to see the floor painted, but it looks very empty, and the rug isn't big enough to hold the space. It should be twice the size at least.'

FINISHING TOUCHES p.228

Project

The designers in Muswell Hill were each given a bevelled mirror to upcycle and incorporate into their design. Adding a wooden frame to a mirror is an inexpensive and fairly simple way to completely change its look.

Geometric decoration.

Chicken wire and keepsakes.

A painted frame.

HOW TO ADD A WOODEN FRAME TO A MIRROR

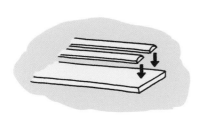

1 Measure the length and height of your mirror to determine how large a frame you need. You can use skirting board together with additional moulding for a layered look. You can get the wood cut to size at the DIY shop. Measure the wood that you want to be your outer piece and mark the measurement on the outer edge.

2 Working inwards from the mark on the outer edge of the wood, cut the wood at a 45° angle; at the opposite end make the 45° cut going in the other direction so the pieces fit together neatly. Continue measuring and cutting all four sides. Sand the wood and then use wood glue to attach the pieces together.

3 Prime and paint the frame and when dry arrange the frame to mount onto your mirror. Glue the middle of the back of each strip of moulding and attach to the mirror. Fill any gaps with paintable caulk and when dry, paint to match.

Decorating details

Now it is time to get down to the nitty gritty: the details of how to furnish and finish off your home. In this section you will find tips and tricks for buying, upcycling and arranging furniture, the lowdown on using fabrics and choosing window treatments, great ideas for delightful displays and, last but by no means least, a few thoughts about finishing touches. The end result? Your house is transformed into a good-looking, practical and comfortable home.

Furniture

Whether you choose designer style or second-hand bargains, aim to buy furniture that is well-made, comfortable and solid. Quality pieces will stand the test of time and give great value for money.

When we furnish a room very few of us start from scratch. Try to include pieces you own and mix with carefully chosen items to complete the look.

Furniture for living

What do you do in your living room? It can be a space for relaxing, reading, entertaining, playing, crafting, even working – so you will need to make sure every single item of furniture works really hard to earn its place. Comfortable seating is your first priority. A pair of sofas that face each other, or perhaps L-shaped modular seating, can be a good-looking and convivial alternative to the traditional three-piece suite, while a single sofa can be supplemented with an interesting chair or two, or even a beanbag or floor cushion. Coffee tables, often seen as essential, take up lots of floor space and can interrupt the flow of movement around the room; you may be better off with side tables, a console table against the back of the sofa, or even a small chest of drawers at one arm, which can double up as useful extra storage space.

In small rooms, look for neat, low pieces, but avoid making everything miniature, or you could end up with a doll's-house effect. In large rooms, generously sized, high-backed furnishings work well. Group them sociably rather than placing them around the edges of the room, which can look somewhat institutional. If you are in any doubt as to how to arrange your furniture, there's a really simple solution: make life-sized paper templates and lay them out on the floor. Simply move them around until everything feels as if it's in its rightful place.

Choosing the perfect sofa

▶ The seat depth and back height should allow you to sit comfortably, neither too slumped nor too upright, and to get up easily.

▶ Look for a frame with smooth, well-fitting joints and no knots, splits or cracks. When you sit down it shouldn't 'give' more than a little.

▶ Cushions should be well stuffed, and seams stitched straight and strong .

▶ A washable loose cover is a good idea if you have children or animals.

▶ Don't overcrowd a small room with a huge sofa. But in a large room, a tiny sofa will disappear.

▶ Will it go through your front door? If your hall is exceptionally narrow, look for a model with removable back, arms and/or legs.

HOW TO DÉCOUPAGE A TABLE TOP p.215

Space-saving furniture

Sofa bed

Perfect for putting up last-minute guests. Before you buy, make sure both the sofa and the mattress are comfortable and hardwearing, and that the opening mechanism is easy to operate.

Extending dining table

One leaf or two? Round, oval, square or rectangular? Traditional or modern? Choose an extending table to make room for dinner parties or family get-togethers.

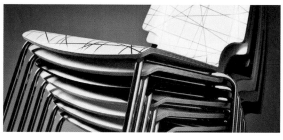

Stacking chairs

For when you need extra seating, chairs that can be stacked away when not in use can be really handy. Or how about a set of stools, which can be pushed under the table tidily?

Nesting side tables

In a small living room it's great to be able to 'nest' side tables together so they take up less floor space when you're not actually using them. These days you can find some up-to-date styles.

Coffee table with storage

Coffee tables inevitably get piled with all sorts of things, so it makes sense to choose one with either a drawer or a shelf beneath. Or use a chest and enjoy capacious storage space.

Hideaway desk

A hinged desk that folds down from the wall is an ideal option for occasional admin. Or you could conceal an entire office in a cleverly designed cupboard or bureau.

Bedrooms

Invest in quality pieces for the bedroom: a great mattress and spacious wardrobes. For kids, function comes first, but have fun, too.

↑ A comfortable bed is the most important item of furniture in the bedroom – and a focal point for decoration.

↗ Bespoke cabin beds are on most kids' wishlists; this one provides a cool hideaway.

A peaceful sanctuary

A comfortable bed and all-encompassing storage are the key components of a bedroom and, from subtle pieces to statement designs; there are all sorts of options to suit any budget. Flat-packs are cheap and can easily be painted and given new handles for a more upmarket appearance (just make sure they're not too flimsy). Second-hand items from junk shops or auctions can be a solid, handsome choice, too. Don't be afraid to make furniture more useful by screwing in hooks, adding shelves or gluing a mirror onto the back of a door.

Child's play

In a child's bedroom, forget themed furniture and choose well-made, simple pieces that will still be useable (even if they have to be given a lick of paint) in decades to come. For younger children, keep furniture around the edges of the room, leaving plenty of play space in the middle. As for teenagers, a homework area is important, as is a chill-out zone with a relaxing chair or beanbag. Add a dressing table (this could double up as the desk), a mirror and, for good organisation, a pin board or magnetic board and some open-topped storage for all those bits and pieces that you'd prefer not to end up on the floor.

→ A grown-up girl's
room with rich colours
and fun features.

A good night's sleep

▶ Choose as big a bed as you can. Disturbance from a partner (or children) is one of the most common causes of sleeping complaints.

▶ The mattress should be comfortable and supportive. Lying down, slide the flat of your hand into the hollow of your back. If it slides in very easily, the bed is too firm; if it's hard to slide your hand in, the bed is too soft.

▶ If you and your partner prefer different mattresses, or are very different in weight, you may need a combination mattress, or two singles that zip together

▶ Launder pillows regularly and replace every few years.

Dining rooms and offices

Anywhere you spend time sitting down – be it a home office or entertaining in a dining room – needs to have furniture that is comfortable as well as attractive.

Are you eating comfortably?

If you entertain a lot (or have a large family) buy the biggest possible dining table in a shape and style that suits your room – or choose one that extends when necessary. As for chairs, aim for a design that suits the height of the table and is both upright and supportive for eating, and comfortable enough for relaxing afterwards.

A stylish study

When working from home, personality is as important as efficiency so, provided they are practical, why not look for more interesting alternatives such as old school lockers, a blackboard resting on a pair of metal filing cabinets, an architect's plan chest or a distressed kitchen dresser? And while it is a good idea to choose a chair on wheels that swivels and is height-adjustable, it doesn't have to be boring black – it could be upholstered in a joyful pattern that will enhance your office. Hunt around auctions, junk shops, markets and the like for home office furniture that you actually find appealing. As long as it's in good condition and suits the space, there are no limits on style.

↑ Traditional writing desks are beautiful pieces of furniture as well as being a useful addition to any family space.

SETTING UP A HOME OFFICE p.133

Creating a great new piece of furniture out of something dull or downtrodden can be as straightforward as a coat of paint, or a change of knobs or handles.

Upcycled furniture and accessories

Turning unloved items of furniture into gorgeous objects of desire is not as challenging as it might sound.

A coat of paint or a new cover will transform many an ugly duckling, and you can even paste wallpaper (or other attractive paper, such as old maps or sheet music) onto the flat panels of furniture to co-ordinate with your new paint job. Alternatively, use mirror or mosaic tiles to cover a boring surface – such as a clean-lined, pine side table. Another simple trick is to change old knobs or handles. Just unscrew the old ones, fill holes as necessary, and attach your lovely new ones.

If you can use a pair of scissors you can cut out and use a piece of sticky-back plastic (now available in plenty of highly desirable patterns) to line a dull chest or wardrobe. The result is not only a smooth, clean surface for your clothes, but also a jolt of visual appeal every time you open the door or drawer. And if you can handle a saw, drill and screwdriver there are all sorts of possibilities, from apple-crate shelving to wheeled-pallet coffee tables. It's all about ingenuity and the willingness to have a go.

One last word: leave anything rare, valuable or antique to the experts and, even then, it's best to stick to essential repairs only.

1930s Suburbia
Surbiton 1930

In the UK 54 million people live in the suburbs – that's 86 per cent of the population. One hundred years ago much of the land that we now regard as suburbs of major cities was undeveloped, but during the inter-war period – the 20 years between 1919 and 1939 – a combination of social and technological factors led to the greatest house-building boom this country has ever seen. In 1919 there were eight million homes in the UK; by 1939 this had risen to more than 12 million.

Berrylands estate near Surbiton in Surrey – nicknamed 'Suburbiton' – is the archetypal development. In 1930 hundreds of new three-bedroom, semi-detached homes were built around four new wide roads, serviced by a new train station, shops, a cinema and lido. This was where the hard-working family aspired to be. Estates like this one are common across the UK, their familiarity inspiring George Orwell to speak of 'the deep, deep sleep of England'.

When they were built these houses were the embodiment of the ideal home. Because they were constructed on undeveloped land they could be generous in size: a far cry from the cramped housing that existed in the polluted cities during the1930s. Semi-detached houses were cheaper to build than detached – and each pair was given enough individuality to set it apart from its neighbours. The doors were moved to the edges of the property to enhance the sense of privacy. Inside was everything people wanted in a modern home – electricity, indoor plumbing, three bedrooms, a generous garden and a sense of light and space. But the exteriors tell a different story. In the 1930s architects were interested in clean-lined Modernism – but the general public wanted the security of 'Old English' or mock Tudor styles. These houses were designed by building firms to satisfy the restrained tastes of the majority and, with high-pitched roofs, curved bay windows and mock-Tudor boarding, they are, from the outside at least, solidly old-fashioned.

▶ The 1930s home was designed to be lighter than say terraced houses, with more space and taller rooms – although in reality most houses were quite dark inside.

▶ By the 1930s in some homes the 'best room' had moved to the rear, thereby allowing it to open onto the spacious garden. Informal space had replaced the traditional drawing room in some houses, but many still had a small sitting room for guests.

▶ Many of the interior features associated with the 'Old English' style – the ceiling rose, the dado rail and elaborate cornicing – had disappeared, although the picture rail usually remained in most rooms (it was still very practical) and the dado rail could still sometimes be found in the hallway.

← Suburban estates, with their grass verges and wide roads, were designed to emulate the wide open spaces found in the countryside.

↗ The rounded bay window is a feature usually seen in Regency architecture.

PERIOD CHARACTER p.9

▶ Ceilings would often be covered with a variety of effects, including false beams, embossed paper or standard whitewash, with many featuring a textured plaster finish to imitate houses of old.

▶ Popular wall coverings included busy wallpapers with floral or (later) geometric patterns, or else plain painted surfaces (unthinkable to the Victorians) were matched with green and leafy borders, giving the impression of a hedgerow bordering the wall. Paints were becoming more popular and more widely available, in a greater range of colours, from pale greens and blues to autumnal reds and browns; duck egg blue started to be used in 1930s bathrooms.

▶ Linoleum was, by now, a standard floor covering – just one of the many modern materials which took hold in the 1930s house. Bakelite was another, an early plastic often used for door knobs and light switches.

CASE STUDY Safari in Suburbia

Bev wanted the feeling of Africa to be part of what she hoped would be a light, spacious and organised living room.

BRIEF

Bev and her family had lived in their house for six and half years and last decorated the front reception room about five years ago. She wanted the room to be more useable as a study/living room/TV room, with more storage and places in which to display personal belongings. She was keen to retain the fireplace and built-in cupboards on either side of the chimney-breast. Bev liked shabby chic style but also wanted the room to feature a nod to her South African heritage with an African feel incorporated into the room. The room was flooded with light from the bay window, and Bev wanted to keep it as light and airy as possible. On her wish list were new curtains, lighting, rugs and renovation or upcycling of her existing furniture.

BEFORE

Sunny space

Pattern and texture

Fabric swatches

Useful storage

→ The designer's proposal included an extensive array of swatches, as well as a photographic impression of storage ideas.

→ Storage files have been covered with the same wallpaper as the feature wall.

▶ The neutral walls keep the room bright and airy, while soft red is used as an accent colour.

▶ Bev's oak floor is shown off to its best advantage against pale walls, but the rug introduces pattern and texture to the room.

▶ A reupholstered and painted second-hand ottoman provides useful storage, and acts as a coffee table in the centre of the room.

▶ The small sofa in the bay means the space is not blocked by large furniture.

▶ A bold agapanthus wallpaper makes a feature of the chimneybreast. Floating shelves have been added either side, faced with picture rail moulding.

AFTER

MAKE THE MOST
OF NATURAL LIGHT
p.123

ORGANISED LIVING
p.126

DESIGN HIGHLIGHT

↘ A mirror at the end of the room reflects light from the window and makes that area brighter.

↑→ Bespoke cushions, featuring some of Africa's 'Big Five', liven up the sofa.

↑ This collection of three plates makes a colourful display.

JUDGE'S VIEW

'The secrétaire, with new handles and painted up, looks great. The room has reached a really high standard. It's beautiful.'

CASE STUDY A Useful Family Space

An under-used space has become a comfortable room for all the family as well as a sociable place for entertaining.

BRIEF

Julia's living room was not being fully utilised – most of the family's socialising happened in the kitchen – so she really wanted it to be turned into a comfortable family living/TV room that could be used for entertaining and was also a place to relax after a long day at work. As her family was arty, creative and loved reading she especially wanted an area for their books incorporated into the design. She favoured purple, green, cream and plum tones, and was keen to have new lighting and for her furniture to be updated.

BEFORE

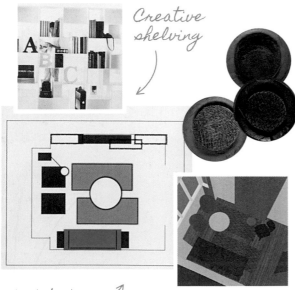

Creative shelving

Rich colours

Updated floor plan

↑ The mood board includes ideas for colour, storage for the family's books and different views of the floor plan.

→ The sofa cushions echo the colours in the patterned curtains.

→ A large
bulb provides
lighting for the
reading area.

▶ The sofa has been reupholstered in two tones of chenille fabric, while a floating shelf is the ideal spot for a TV.

▶ The assymetrical shelving unit fills a corner of the room; different shelf sizes make it interesting as well as useful. Concealed LED lighting adds to the effect.

▶ The wooden floor has been softened with two woven rugs.

▶ Brightly coloured soft furnishings and accessories add to the effect.

▶ The coffee table is made from reclaimed timber and is painted in the same fresh green as the walls.

▶ The TV is now conveniently sited in an alcove, with a storage basket for DVDs tucked underneath.

AFTER

CASE STUDY | A Natural Haven

A place to escape that included elements of the natural world was the brief for the design of this living room.

BRIEF

Celia and her family had not decorated their house since they moved in two years ago. She wanted a restful, peaceful and grown-up living room: a child-free zone where she and her husband could relax after work. She envisaged a sophisticated and elegant drawing room with a feature fireplace, built-in furniture and maximum storage space. It was also important that there was enough space and seating for Celia and her husband to entertain friends in the evenings and at weekends. They both liked natural fabrics, materials and textures, such as wicker, wool, leather, wood and stone. The carpet needed replacing and they wanted some new lighting and furniture.

BEFORE

Soft colours and natural textures

A mixture of styles

→ The designer's mood board contains examples of pattern and fabric choices, as well as furniture ideas.

▶ The carpet has been taken up and new oak laminate boards laid, giving the natural finish Celia was hoping for.

▶ The soft lilac walls co-ordinate with the new floor and make the room feel like a grown-up space.

▶ A single low, sleek shelf runs the length of the room and creates a contemporary feel.

▶ New chairs sit under the window to provide the additional seating Celia wanted.

▶ Contrasting styles of lighting have been used here: a traditional chandelier and a modern arc light.

→ The white-painted coffee table is clean, and modern with storage underneath.

↓ The finished room is sleek and contemporary with traditional touches.

AFTER

HOW TO SAND
FLOORBOARDS
p.115

DESIGN HIGHLIGHT
↓ ↘ Hand-knitted cushions add a rustic texture, while patterned fabrics are pretty and elegant.

↓ The metal-framed fireplace has been filled with flowers and candles. The artwork above echoes its colour and shape, making it even more of a focal point.

↑ A new floating cupboard fills an alcove and provides much-needed storage.

JUDGE'S VIEW
'The new unit works so well, and the shelf takes your eye sinuously through the room. It forms a mantle and makes more sense of the small fireplace.'

ACCESSORIES
p.202

Project

The designers at Surbiton were each given a ceramic vase to upcycle and incorporate into their design. Adding a mosaic to a plain ceramic piece is sure to add flair and individuality.

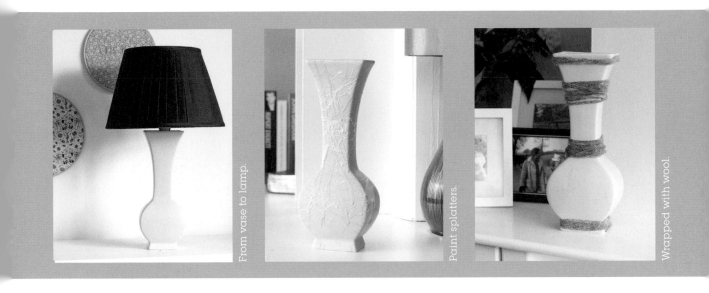

From vase to lamp.

Paint splatters.

Wrapped with wool.

HOW TO ADD A MOSAIC DESIGN TO A CERAMIC VASE

1 First plan your design and collect your mosaic tiles. You can buy these from craft shops or even use old pieces of broken crockery. Wash and dry the vase to remove grease and dust. Cover the back of each tile with silicone adhesive and start to create your mosaic. Once complete the vase needs to dry for at least 12 hours.

2 Mix some grout according to the instructions on the packet and press into the spaces between the tiles using a craft stick to avoid cutting your fingers on sharp edges.

3 Leave to dry for about 10 minutes and remove any excess grout by buffing gently with a damp sponge; repeat as necessary. Let the vase dry for another 12 hours, clean it again and then bring up the shine with a dry cloth.

Soft furnishings

From the softest cashmere to the hardest-wearing denim, you can create your own, individual look and style with irresistible soft furnishings.

Patterned, textured or plain, subtle or spectacular, fabrics can transform a room. But picking the right fabric for covering a sofa or making a blind can be a tricky business. While budget, personal taste and the overall decoration of the room are key factors, they're not the only considerations. From a practical point of view, it is important to match the fabric to the intended project. So, before you start, make sure you know your silks from your synthetics and your cottons from your corduroys.

How to choose fabric

▶ Always ask for a swatch or, even better, borrow or buy a length of fabric so you can see how it will look in situ.

▶ Wider fabric is often better value. Less sewing may be required, too.

▶ Heavier fabrics are usually too bulky for small projects; lighter fabrics tend to wear more quickly.

▶ Check how the fabric is categorised: for light, general or heavy domestic use. And look for 'rub test' figures – 16,000 or above is suitable for general domestic use.

▶ Is it washable, and at what temperature? Will it shrink?

▶ Large patterns require more fabric so that you can match the repeats, and can end up being much more expensive than plains or small patterns.

How are fabrics made?

Fabrics are composed of natural or synthetic fibres, or blends of them. They can be plain or woven with a pattern. Printing is done by machine or by hand, or digitally using computer technology (which allows small, personalised runs). Most fabrics are available in a variety of weights.

Fibres

▶ **Cotton:** Ranging from lightweight muslin to heavy canvas, cotton dyes and prints well, and is easy to care for.

▶ **Linen:** It has a lovely drape and lustre, but linen creases easily (so is often mixed with other fibres).

▶ **Nylon, or polyamide:** Man-made fibres are tough and resist abrasion, but tend to produce static electricity.

▶ **Polyester:** This is a very strong synthetic fibre that mixes well with other fibres. It can be washed frequently and on high temperatures.

▶ **Silk:** It comes in intense colours and has an attractive, lustrous surface, but silk is delicate.

▶ **Viscose:** Made from wood pulp, viscose is hardwearing and durable.

▶ **Wool:** Breathable, warm and naturally water-resistant, wool varies from heavy sheep's wool to fine cashmere. It will shrink and felt if washed and spun at too high a temperature.

▶ **Oilcloth:** This is cotton that has been coated with a PVC resin or acrylic to make it waterproof. Although durable and wipeable, it can stain and isn't heat-resistant.

A quick guide to weaves

Bouclé has a looped pile.

Corduroy features pile in stripes.

Damasks contrast matt and shiny areas of pattern; usually rather traditional.

Jacquards feature a complex, raised pattern.

Moiré has a watermark pattern; often on silks.

Satin is a heavy with a lustrous surface, usually in silk or polyester.

Twill weave produces diagonal or zigzag lines on the surface.

Velvet may be made from a variety of fibres and features a luxurious, soft pile.

↖↑ Don't be afraid to experiment with different fabrics. Contrasts in colour, pattern and texture can be delightful.

VARIETIES OF TEXTURE p.41

Upholstery

Choose fabrics wisely and you will get the best from them. For covering sofas and chairs, there's an endless choice of colours, patterns and textures, but practicality is important, too.

Hardwearing, tightly woven fabrics are the best choice for most upholstered furniture, though in some cases (a seldom-used bedroom chair, for example) a more decorative fabric, such as silk, is fine. Medium- to heavy-weight cottons and cotton mixes, linen mixes and wools are all good choices, while corduroy, denim and low-pile velvet have appealing textures and should be long-lasting. Avoid deep piles, which may become crushed, and loose or loopy weaves, which are likely to catch and snag.

Upholstering with plains is pretty straightforward, but make sure that any nap runs in the same direction when all the pieces are made up. Stripes should run straight and be aligned and, if you choose a bold pattern, you will need to centre the motifs on sofa or chair backs, seats and cushions (this can mean buying a lot of fabric). For new and replacement upholstery and loose covers, whatever fabric you choose should usually be fire-retardant, though it is sometimes possible to use a non-fire retardant fabric over a fire-retardant interlining – always check with the manufacturer or retailer.

Loose covers

A great way to give a new lease of life to any fabric-covered furniture, from a sofa to a dining chair, loose covers can also be used to alter a piece's proportions and even its overall character. Style-wise, they can be sleek and chic, casually unstructured or frilly and flouncy – depending on how they are cut and whether they are designed with a zip or ties, pleats or gathers, piping or a valance. Pick a fabric that is washable, and substantial enough to hold its shape yet soft enough to be comfortable; medium-weight cottons, linens or blends, or light wools, are all ideal.

PATTERN p.36

← Fresh upholstery makes a radical difference to old furniture.

→↓ It is relatively easy to make a new cover for a beanbag, or to re-cover a seat, box lid or stool.

Recovering seats, boxes and beanbags

Take the seat out of the chair frame and carefully remove the old covering. Lay the seat onto your fabric, positioning it carefully so that any pattern is centred or aligned. Draw about 10cm (4in) around the seat and cut the fabric out, then use a staple gun to attach it – quite taut but not overly stretched – first at the centre of each side, then at the corners, and then in-between. Make sure the fabric is even and the corners are neat. Drop the seat back into the frame and re-attach. To re-cover the padded lid of a box, remove its hinges and treat as a chair seat. Screw the hinges back on and re-attach. Give a bean bag a new lease of life with a replacement cover. Remove the old cover (leaving the filling in the liner) and take it apart, then use it as a template to cut out your new fabric. Stitch together securely, adding a zip, hook-and-loop tape or other form of fastening.

Accessories

Both practical and beautiful, soft furnishings create a unique sense of personal style. Use them in every room of your home.

Cushions

A new cushion will instantly brighten up a boring sofa or chair and add visual interest to a room – use the colour and pattern either to pull a scheme together or create a dynamic contrast. It's easy to make your own cushion cover – or, if sewing's not your thing, inexpensive to have them made for you. You can use almost any fabric, within reason and, as you will only need a small amount, you can go for something quite luxurious – a square metre should make four average sized cushion fronts, then you can use cheaper fabric for the back. Alternatively, try pieces of vintage fabric for an eclectic look, and have fun with different shapes, sizes, trims and fastenings.

Table linen

For tablecloths, runners and napkins, light to medium weight cottons, linens and cotton or linen blends are best. Damasks are a traditional choice,

and a hand-embroidered tablecloth can look very pretty. But above all, if you are going to use them every day, choose fabrics that will withstand frequent washing, reserving the delicates for special occasions. For the last word in ease of cleaning, your best bet is oilcloth, a plastic-coated cloth that simply wipes down with a damp cloth and comes in a massive range of gorgeous colours and patterns.

Throws and bedspreads

If you want to transform a bedroom in an instant, simply make up the bed in plain white linens and cover it with a stunning bedspread. Change the cover whenever you wish for an instant injection of colour and pattern – eiderdowns, quilts, blankets and throws are just as versatile, of course. The same applies to your sofa: tuck a throw, blanket or other length of fabric neatly over it – back, seat, arms or all over – for a fresh (and inexpensive) new look.

MAKING A HOUSE A HOME p.230

Choosing bed linen

Quality bed linen will not only feel more comfortable, but will wash well and last for years.

▶ **Cotton:** Hardwearing, easy to clean and breathable, cotton is a popular choice, and pure Egyptian cotton is considered the finest. Styles include percale, satin, sateen, waffle, jacquard, flannel, jersey and corduroy.

▶ **Artificial fibres:** Fibres like viscose and rayon are soft, durable and absorbent, but may shrink when washed.

▶ **Synthetics:** Polyester, acrylic and nylon are great for resisting creases, but can make you uncomfortably hot.

▶ **Blends:** These include polycotton, and can offer an ideal combination of the qualities of two or more fibres.

▶ **Linen:** Breathable with a cool, crisp touch, linen gets softer as it gets older – but it does need a lot of ironing.

▶ **Silk:** Also highly breathable, silk will keep you warm in winter and cool in summer; it's even said to reduce wrinkles and make your hair glossy. It needs gentle handling.

↖↑ Adding cushions gives you the chance to experiment with bright colours and interesting patterns.

← Layer a bed with quilts, throws and cushions for a luxurious and co-ordinated look.

Art Deco Houses
Beckenham 1934

Art Deco was the world's first truly international style – incorporating elements of European Art Nouveau, Parisian Art Deco, British Arts and Crafts and the designs of American Jazz Modern. It formed part of the larger Modernist Movement that infused everything from literature and art to political thought and architecture, and offered a bright future for the people of the post-industrial age.

Famously backward looking in their designs, British architects did not embrace the Art Deco style for much domestic architecture, though it can be seen in the elegant department stores, cinemas, hotels and theatres built in the 1920s and 1930s. However, at the Ideal Home Exhibition of 1934, the 'Village of Tomorrow' was unveiled, featuring nine different examples of Art Deco homes. It appealed to some forward thinking developers, and there was a short-lived wave of Art Deco building, especially in the South East and the Midlands – areas where new automotive and electrical industries were attracting young people with comfortable employment.

These five houses were built in 1934, during a new era of home ownership and the expansion of the middle classes that took place after the First World War. The white, box-like architecture with crisp horizontal lines, broken by vertical columns and large windows and doors, mimics the work of contemporary artists such as Mondrian.

▶ The exterior walls are clad in white concrete or 'snowcrete', designed to reflect the sun and keep the inside cool. They must be painted every two years to maintain their pristine condition.

▶ Long lines of windows were designed to let as much light into the house as possible. It was a feature that architects in 1934 recognised as 'having a beneficial effect upon the health of the occupants'.

▶ The 'best rooms', previously at the front of the house, were moved to the back- away from the road. This increased privacy also meant that best rooms would open onto the spacious garden. More informal living rooms replaced formal spaces, but many houses still had a small sitting room just for guests.

▶ Parquet flooring, with its elegant finish and geometric style, was a popular floor covering in 1930s housing. Linoleum or vinyl tiles in geometric or monochrome patterns were also popular.

▶ Rather than the fitted kitchens we have today, many pieces in an Art Deco kitchen would have been freestanding, the major exception being the pantry, which became smaller between the wars as tinned food became popular.

▶ Although coal fires were still a necessity for many houses, chimneys in Art Deco houses were much less prominent than in previous styles. In these houses the chimney comes up through the sunroof, leaving little of the stack exposed.

← The iconic Art Deco triangular detail was influenced by Aztec design and created in plaster.

→ These houses copy elements of American Art Deco beach houses: white walls to keep the inside cool, sunrooms and flat roofs.

PERIOD
CHARACTER p.9

1930s Beach Hut

A love of Miami was the starting point for this room that mixes Art Deco, traditional pieces and shabby chic.

BRIEF

Rachel and Sue's sunroom (a modern extension rather than the original room) was a playroom for Sue's grandchildren and used for storage. They wanted their redesigned room to capture the Art Deco spirit of Miami and to give them their dream of a 'beach hut in the sky'. The room needed to be dual purpose: a place to socialise in and somewhere to retreat and read books or watch films. The bulky furniture didn't help the functionality or look of the room. Their favoured palette included cream, pale green and light purples, rather than bold colours or gold, and they wanted to avoid anything twee or kitsch.

BEFORE

→ The designer's vision focuses on the colour palette as well as photographic ideas. Also included are pieces of furniture that could be incorporated into the design.

Vintage furniture

Antique mirror

Colour and room set inspirations

→ The frame wall was a stand-out feature in this design scheme.

▶ The soft green walls complement the dark wood furniture and plum-coloured sofa.

▶ The grouped artwork and mirrors with mismatched frames are hung at the same level as the two windows, allowing the eye to travel the length of the wall.

▶ The driftwood shelving, palm wallpaper and retro glassware gives the room the Miami beach feel that Rachel and Sue wanted.

▶ The entertaining space is filled with unique, upcycled furniture.

↓→ The elegant sideboard doubles up as a drinks cabinet and the driftwood shelves are used for storing cocktail accessories.

AFTER

Decadent Art Deco

The clients wanted their sunroom and terrace to be an adult-only space for relaxing and entertaining, both inside and out.

BRIEF

Kathryn and Roy had been meticulously restoring their home for seven years, and wanted someone to bring the Art Deco look to their sunroom and terrace. They wanted a room that felt decadent and grown up, which would be off limits to their two young sons, and that Roy could use as a workspace when needed. They loved the colours and materials that encapsulate the Art Deco era: glass, white, black, silver and emerald green, but they were happy with the idea of introducing other colours to these rooms, perhaps on a wall or as a window dressing. There were also two 1930s chairs that could be reupholstered.

BEFORE

1930s bar

Art Deco seating

Drinks cabinet

→ The designer's mood board shows that the client's brief has been listened to: it includes ideas, inspiration, sketches and a floorplan.

JUDGE'S VIEW

'The green is perfect – so Deco and also so now. The furniture is arranged in a very inviting way. The room is nicely thought-through.'

▶ The sleek Art Deco cocktail bar and terrace are decorated in rich emerald and monochrome colours.

▶ Kathryn's Art deco armchairs have been covered in sumptuous fabrics, and the designer has added cushions with a lavish design that contrasts with the clean lines of the rest of the colour scheme.

▶ A large rug in soft, neutral tones has been added to the seating area and echoes the geometric lines elsewhere in the room.

▶ A curved monochrome bar – at the top of Roy's wish list – takes pride of place.

▶ The designer also upcycled a console table in black and white to add another monochrome element to the scheme.

→ An interesting display livens up the monochrome console table.

AFTER

↓ The dark stained decking and painted furniture carry the monochrome scheme from the inside to the outside.

→ A bright green area of grass contrasts with the dark decking and white painted walls, once again echoing the colour scheme of the interior.

↑ The painted garden furniture ties in with the overall colour scheme.

→ A glossy black curved bar and emerald-green paintwork perfectly fit the Art Deco brief.

JUDGE'S VIEW
'The high-street lanterns give a wink to the Deco style, but gathering them together would have created a more powerful display.'

CASE STUDY

1950s Workspace

Nigel and Heather wanted to bring a touch of vibrancy to a cluttered office and create a terrace they could both enjoy.

BRIEF

The sunroom was used as an office for Nigel, but had become a bit of a dumping ground. It felt cramped, with dated furniture. Although the room needed to remain as an office, Nigel was keen for it to be decluttered and given a fresh approach, with clever storage solutions, desk space, seating and good lighting. Bright sunlight was a problem when working, so blinds were also on his wish list. Heather liked every shade of green and Nigel favoured bold colour and clean lines; they both loved retro designs. Out on the terrace Nigel and Heather wanted some soft planting and outdoor lighting.

BEFORE

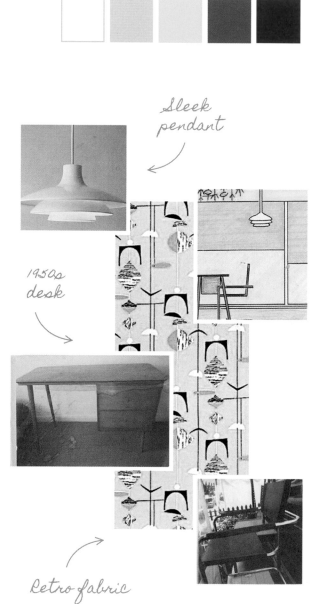

Sleek pendant

1950s desk

Retro fabric

→ The designer's proposal incorporates bright colours and the retro style favoured by Nigel and Heather, with ideas for both inside and out.

▶ Roller blinds are essential for working in this very bright room. They are headed by a pelmet covered in a bold, retro fabric.

▶ The glass desk appears to take up virtually no room, and floats on inexpensive trestle legs.

▶ Bright yellow is used as an accent colour throughout the room, including on the filing cabinets and cupboard fronts.

▶ New shelving houses Nigel's printer and provides more storage for paperwork. The white shelves blend in with the wall colour.

→ Floating shelves provide space to store Nigel's office essentials.

↓ The arms of the vintage metal chair have been covered with the same fabric as the window pelmet.

AFTER

← Floor-to-ceiling storage clears clutter out of the room.

← The retro light fitting complements the rest of the office furniture.

↓ New cushion covers and a mirror-topped table refresh the roof terrace.

DESIGN HIGHLIGHT
↓ Plain roller blinds are inexpensive – the patterned pelmet adds interest.

JUDGE'S VIEW
'The decking does link nicely with inside, but overall I don't get it. It's not a garden design.'

BLINDS p.220

Project

The designers in Beckenham were given a white cube to upcycle. Gluing paper cut-outs, or découpage, is a great way to transform a flat surface.

Découpage using 1930s images.

A mirror top with an Art Deco-style edge.

Another mirror top with clean lines.

HOW TO DÉCOUPAGE A TABLE TOP

1 If your table top has a shiny surface, sand the surface flat to make a good key for your paper to stick to. Brush away any dust.

2 You can use any sort of paper for découpage but make sure it is not too thick or flimsy; cut it into 8cm (3¼in) squares. Brush PVA glue onto the table top and smooth your squares of paper on top. You can overlap with other pieces of paper, but ensure that all edges have glue on them. When your images reach the edges, glue the sides of the table and splice the paper to avoid bunching around curved edges. Straight edge furniture can be wrapped over the edges without cutting.

3 Apply two or more thin layers of varnish over all the decoupage areas, remembering to leave to dry for the correct time between coats.

Window treatments

Practical as well as pretty, curtains, blinds and shutters are an important feature in every room.

Window treatments are often necessary for privacy, and may help with insulation, soundproofing and even security, but they are much more than just a functional addition to a room. A well designed set of curtains, blinds or shutters will complement the overall design scheme – and can correct a badly proportioned window, disguise an unattractive view, filter bright light, provide a visual link between inside and out and, in general, give the space a satisfyingly 'finished' feel.

Before you start, establish your priorities. If your window treatment is there purely to keep out prying eyes, an inexpensive blind or muslin café curtain may be just the thing – or even stick-on window film, easy to apply, cheap and available in a variety of different patterns. Save money where possible,

because professionally made, lavish window treatments can be costly (though they should last a long time). For light control, blinds and louvered shutters are better than traditional curtains, while layered window treatments – curtains as well as shutters, perhaps – can give you more options. Consider whether you would like 'extras' such as pelmets, tie backs and the like – they may give a more sophisticated look, but costs can soon mount up. And make sure each window treatment really suits the space: we are talking durable shutters or hard-wearing fabric curtains in children's rooms and sitting rooms, splashproof blinds in kitchens and bathrooms and silk curtains in bedrooms, for example. Once you have made the basic decisions, there are a wonderful variety of styles from which to choose.

MAKE THE MOST OF NATURAL LIGHT p.123

Instant window treatments

Lace panel

A pretty way to provide privacy. Use vintage lace for an interesting effect. Muslin is a plainer, but value-for-money alternative.

Sari fabric

Gorgeous colours and patterns, sometimes including metallic thread, make this a very decorative option for dressing windows.

Blanket

A lightweight blanket will drape well over a large window or can be turned into a blind. There are plain and patterned options.

Lightweight rug

Punch eyelet holes in the rug and thread over a sturdy pole, and you have instant pattern and colour.

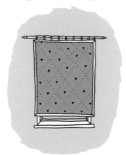

Small quilt / bedcover / throw

Think laterally and use bed coverings as window treatments. Large and already hemmed, they can be just the ticket.

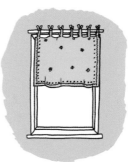

Tablecloth

There are all sorts of options, from embroidered to gingham to plain. Inexpensive, quick and easy.

Curtains

Choosing and fitting curtains is more than a matter of finding beautiful fabric that will enhance your room – you'll need to consider their length and style, and how they will be hung, too.

Fabric
Curtains can be made from practically any fabric. The heavier the fabric, the better it will hold a fold, although very heavy fabrics will be too bulky for small windows (and require a sturdy track or pole). Light fabrics can look floppy unless they are lined, and will let daylight through.

Linings
Linings are essential on all but sheers to help curtains hang neatly and protect them from fading, dirt and condensation. Blackout linings are ideal in a bedroom that gets sun in the mornings, while thermal linings can be as effective as double-glazing.

Length and width
To let maximum light into the room, fit a pole or track that overhangs far enough each side to allow the curtains to be drawn right away from the window – bearing in mind that full, thick curtains need more 'stack back' space than light, thin ones. Floor length curtains are generally better than sill-length, although shorter curtains may suit the space better when radiators or window seats are in the way.

← Extra-long curtains give a sumptuous look.

↓ Vertical stripes can make a small room appear bigger.

Headings and hangings

The way in which a curtain hangs is determined by its heading, often created by a tape sewn onto the back of the curtain and pulled to form gathers or pleats. For a less formal look, options include tab- and tie-tops (often found on ready-made curtains, but fiddly to draw), a deep hem that slides over a pole, large eyelets, clips (magnetic ones are easy to use) or even just some hooks.

Poles, tracks, wires and rods

The most straightforward way to hang curtains is from a pole, though you need some clearance above and below for it to look right. Finished with plain or decorative finials, poles are designed to be on show. Tracks, on the other hand, are more subtle. Made from plastic (cheap) or metal (smart), they can be mounted either on the wall or ceiling; they also bend around bay windows. Double tracks allow you to hang both sheers or nets and thicker curtains neatly. On narrow windows or dormers, portiere (swing-arm) rods are an alternative to fixed poles, while for a modern effect you could use tension wire, fixed taut within the window opening.

Blinds

Perfect for smaller rooms where grand window treatments are not quite so appropriate, blinds are also great for modern spaces where you want an understated style – and, because they need far less fabric, they tend to be a lot cheaper than curtains. If you are handy with a sewing machine, you may even be able to make them yourself.

▶ **Roller blinds** are the most basic style, while roll-up blinds, tied with tape or ribbon, have a pretty yet still simple look.

▶ **Roman blinds**, which pull up into soft, wide pleats, are smart and versatile, suiting almost every room. When choosing fabric, opt for something that is mid-weight and not too textured, as blinds need to roll or fold easily against themselves. But there is nothing to stop you combining more than one colour or pattern, in the form of smart, contrast borders down the sides or along the bottom of the blind. And sometimes it's a good idea to combine a plain and a sheer fabric, to allow light through at the top of the window while giving privacy beneath.

▶ **Plain blinds** can be boosted with a good-looking pull (think leather, glass, raffia, stone or rope) or trim (such as ribbon, pom-poms, ric-rac, stitching, fringing, shells or buttons). If you want a dressier look, add curtains as well.

▶ **Venetian blinds** in wood, metal or plastic give a modern look and are a good way to add privacy and let in light at the same time.

↓ Roman blinds are always smart and are a neat way to cover a bay window.

Shutters

Good-looking in an unfussy kind of way, shutters suit both old and new properties. They are expensive but, on the plus side, they are good at blocking out sound and light, and can even provide extra security. The plainest shutters feature a timber frame and solid centre panel (a local joiner should be able to make them for you). Louvred versions (from specialist shutter companies) offer privacy while also controlling the light. Both types can be left as natural wood, or painted whatever colour you like. They can be made as a pair, bi- or tri-fold or in other groupings, either full- or half-height, or one set above another, and fitted within a reveal or to fold back against the walls. For a striking and modern effect, opt for shutters made from opaque or coloured acrylic. Elegant, with a modern edge, they are translucent, so may need to be combined with blinds for night-time privacy.

↑ Shutters fold back completely to let the maximum amount of light into a room.

↖ Roller blinds are simple and work well in kitchens.

Displays

Make the most of your prized possessions by creating beautiful, eye-catching displays.

Displays on walls

A wall is the ideal blank canvas for a display of almost any type. Paintings, collages, drawings, photographs and other flat works of art are the obvious choice – there are so many possibilities that it's easy to cater for any taste and style of interior. Surprisingly, single pictures can be the hardest to hang. Look for convenient alcoves or small walls, as they tend to get lost on their own on a large wall. Pairs of pictures often make more visual sense, while a group of four (two-up, two-down) is smart and sassy.

But why stop at pictures? Textile wall hangings create just as impressive an effect, whether they be gorgeous silk robes, wool tapestries, woven rugs or a good-looking scarf, shawl or banner. And for a really bold display, you can't beat a wall-mounted three-dimensional object. Something as simple as a line of vintage plates can be really decorative, while hanging up your collection of baskets, handbags, shoe lasts, hats, toy cars and so on is a great way to store them and show them off at the same time.

How to arrange a group of pictures

Pictures that are all the same size and identically framed look amazing hung in regular rows. But it's harder to hang less coordinated pictures. A good method is to lay them out on the floor, with the largest picture near the centre, then stand on a chair to look down and get a sense of how the grouping works. Rearrange as necessary, taking out any pictures that jar. You may also find that some need reframing to work in the group. Avoid hanging pictures in ascending or descending sizes.

↗ A grouping of four pictures, displayed with mathematical symmetry, is highly effective.

Choosing the right frame for your picture

A mount, cut at an angle to lead the eye into the picture, looks professional and can bring out key colours (though if in doubt, choose off-white). As for frames, choose a style that is in proportion to your picture and complements it without dominating. In general, black, white and silver frames work well with monochrome or muted pictures, and pale frames work best with pale pictures. Dark frames can enhance brightly coloured artwork.

How to hang a picture

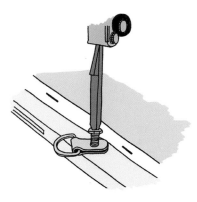

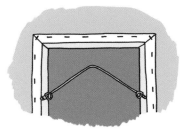

1 Prepare your picture by making two small holes in the back of the frame at each side, about a third of the way down. Attach screw eyes or D-rings.

2 Stretch a length of cord, twine or picture wire between the fastenings. The latter is best for heavy pictures as it won't stretch or fray. Knot it securely, allowing a little slack, but not so much that the cord shows above the picture when hung.

3 What's your wall made from? You can easily bang a nail into timber, and sometimes a picture hook or multiple-pin hook will work on other types of wall, provided the picture is pretty light.

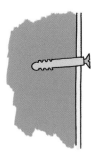

4 For heavy pictures that you want to hang on a stone, brick, plasterboard or breezeblock wall, you will need to drill a hole and use a suitable wall plug with a screw. Check the wall for hidden pipes or cables before you drill or hammer.

5 As a general rule, centre a single picture above a sofa, fireplace or table, or within the wall space. Hang with its horizontal centre at eye level (about 145cm/57in is usually recommended) – unless you feel it looks better another way. This is not an exact science, after all.

Displays in shelves, alcoves and cabinets

The simplest, most obvious and often most effective way to create a display is by placing objects on a shelf, table, mantelpiece or windowsill, in an alcove or within a cabinet, niche or cubbyhole. Poised and deliberate or delightfully informal, these displays are versatile, space-saving and usually easy to arrange.

What are your options? Well, almost anything can be displayed in this way, from cut-glass perfume bottles to books to pebbles from the beach. Fragile or valuable items are best kept up high or behind glazed doors, of course, and you should avoid putting objects where they will simply become an obstruction (interfering with a blind or taking up space on a coffee table, for example). Consider where they will be relation to eye level, and ensure that the most interesting features of your display will definitely be visible. Beyond that, enjoy arranging

and re-arranging your objects until they suit your style and enhance your space.

The art of display

▶ Small objects need to be 'framed' in their surroundings or they will get lost. Large objects can dominate, and need space to breathe. Ensure your displays are proportionate to the space they're in.

▶ Try placing a mirror behind a three-dimensional object on a shelf, so you can see its back, too.

▶ Pairs of items are visually very strong. Place them evenly and symmetrically for maximum impact.

▶ When displaying groups, an uneven number of items is usually more visually appealing.

▶ What shape does your display make? Stand back, squint, and try to see an overall outline, rather than lots of individual objects.

▶ Link groups of objects in a display by shape, size, colour and/or texture. Otherwise they can look incoherent.

▶ Striking ways to display objects include under Victorian glass domes, in printers' trays, test tubes or flower pots, hung from pegs or over a small ladder, up stairs or thrown over a bust or mannequin. Get creative and express yourself.

▶ Lighting will always enhance a display, whether it's natural light falling through a window, a specially fitted spotlight or a table lamp placed nearby.

↑ Colourful displays can add interest to simple kitchen schemes.

← Displaying objects in glass domes is a way to unify groups of very different items.

↖ Grouping items in different ways on shelves adds variety to a display.

Brutalism
Bethnal Green 1950s

'Brutalism' is a term that was attributed to British architect Alison Smithson in 1952, the same year that Le Corbusier designed what is regarded as the first Brutalist building in Marseilles in France. The term Brutalism is derived from the French 'Breton Brut' – meaning raw concrete.

This type of architecture can be identified by its repetitive, angular geometries: a rough, block-like appearance, in some cases with structural support columns and services such as lift shafts on the exterior. Construction is typically made from poured, board-marked concrete, a system of moulding concrete structures using wooden boards, and the surfaces of many of these buildings feature a wood-patterned finish.

As a style Brutalism embodied several ideas about style and function: efficiency, new materials, lack of ornamentation, clarity and integrity. This is a far cry from most people's image of British Brutalism, which we associate with failed post-war attempts to build new communities and 'streets in the sky'.

Keeling House in Bethnal Green, East London, is an example of cluster block housing where multiple separate sections are connected by a shared access space or column – lift-shafts in Keeling House's case. This minimises the amount of shared space and increases the privacy of each flat.

Critics of Brutalism believe that the style reflects the moral breakdown of architecture in the Western world, where dull and soulless structures were imposed on the public by government officials. But Keeling House's architect, Denys Lasdun, who also designed the National Theatre on London's South Bank, didn't see himself as a Brutalist: he saw himself as more of a traditional architect continuing a line of British design that had begun with Christopher Wren.

Inspired by the ideas of the time, Lasdun followed his own path and experimented with combining Brutalist forms of architectural design with modern theories of community. He didn't want to see London filled with identikit tower blocks that had no connection with local history, city planning or architecture.

Constructed between 1957 and 1959 on the site of bomb-damaged terraces, Keeling House was built as council housing to replace workers' cottages and Victorian slums damaged in the Blitz. Lasdun hoped that his design would preserve the idea of neighbourliness that Victorian terraces provided, while giving residents the benefits of modern design and modern materials. He also incorporated communal spaces containing drying areas and greenery where he envisioned neighbours meeting up and chatting.

Keeling House remained Council-owned until 1992, when its poor structural condition meant it was no longer safe for habitation. Saved from demolition by a Grade II listing in 1993 – the first post-war modern building to have one – the building was bought by private developers from Tower Hamlets Council in 1997 for £1.3m, and transformed into a high-rise des-res.

← The use of white on the façade mimics the Art Deco style.

↗ Lasdun experimented with different designs to create a building that would give each living area as much exposure to the sun as possible.

When Keeling House was given its new lease of life in the 1990s, architect Denys Lasdun was invited to help redesign the front lobby, one of the last projects he was involved with. This building is now lauded as one of the most successful conversions of social housing into luxury apartments designed for modern living. These sought-after properties are now worth well in excess of £400,000, a long way from their original purpose as functional, social housing for the less wealthy and less demanding post-war generations.

▶ The redevelopment turned a dingy, dilapidated council block into a 'shiny, chic' private residence, with 'large windows, wooden floors, open-plan living areas, and terraces with big views'.

▶ The living areas were opened out, creating an airy, wood-floored space that appears to be very 'Scandinavian modern': a style popular in minimalist 1960s houses.

▶ The strange shape of the rooms results from an attempt to increase the space while retaining the pipework and electrical cables, and load-bearing concrete pillars.

▶ Most of the internal walls are not load bearing and can easily be removed.

▶ The bedroom floors are made of timber rather than concrete in an attempt to reduce the weight of the overall building.

Finishing touches

When the structural work is done, your walls are finished, your floors are down and the major pieces of furniture are in the right place, it's time to add the details that show off your personality and flair.

Thoughtful final touches add an extra decorative element that really demonstrates who you are. What's more, they are not terribly expensive and can be changed quickly and easily – perhaps with the seasons, or just when you feel like a new look. A few bits and pieces will do the trick. A throw over the arm of a sofa or the back of an armchair is wonderfully appealing, for example, and brings character to even the most boring piece of upholstery. A scattering of cushions – be they square, round, rectangular, bolster-shaped, and featuring piping, buttons or pom pom trims – has the same effect. A group of vases on a shelf; a row of candles on a mantelpiece; a wicker basket or a coloured plastic tub; a characterful lamp, a carved wooden bowl, a ceramic pot, a pretty mirror – it's not hard to see how all sorts of gorgeous accessories, thoughtfully put together, can be the making of a most attractive and interesting room.

↑ Glass jars make simple and inexpensive vases that show off flowers to their best advantage.

The handmade revolution

Anyone with an eye on the latest lifestyle trends is bound to have noticed that there's a huge craft revival happening.

Never have traditional handicrafts such as knitting, crochet, sewing and felting been so popular. Why? Mostly it's because hand-made items, with all their quirky unevenness, are, quite simply, incredibly appealing. In a room where most things are, by necessity, made by machine: regular, even and – dare we say it – sometimes bland, a handmade piece adds a vital element of personality, humanity and soul.

How can you incorporate craft in your home? Well, you can find all sorts of gorgeous hand-made items at craft fairs, online or in specialist shops. Some things are incredibly good value, but don't expect craft to be cheap – the time, materials and skill involved often makes it more expensive than mass-produced items. But remember that you are getting a unique and beautiful piece that you will value forever, rather than something instant, commonplace and throwaway.

If you want to have a go yourself, there is nothing like the satisfaction of learning a new skill – with the added pleasure that you can use the results of your efforts, whether you have made a lamp base or a patchwork quilt, a cushion cover or a mosaic tile, around your home. Craft has never been so cool, and help is at hand all around, in the form of books, courses, classes and online videos.

↑↓ Découpage is a great way to update tables, chairs and cupboards.

↙↓ Creating bespoke pieces is a satisfying way to furnish your home.

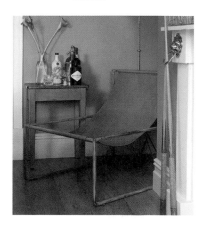

HOW TO DÉCOUPAGE A TABLE TOP p.215

Making a house a home

What's the difference between four walls and a roof, and a place that is welcoming, nurturing and an all-round great place to be? Well, the former is a house and the latter is a home.

A house may look really smart, but a home is where you kick off your shoes, cook up a storm, cuddle the kids, make a mess, laugh, cry and generally live your life. So, while there are plenty of decorating guidelines to help you put together a picture-perfect house, remember that, in creating a home, you should do what suits you best. If you can create a comfortable space for family and friends who fill the house with fun and laughter, you have that wonderful thing: a happy home.

↑ Personal touches are an important part of room design: 'lekker' is Africaans for 'great'.

Decorating with all your senses

In a truly comfortable home, every room is as relaxing and welcoming as it is stylish. It looks right but, just as importantly, it feels right in every way. It could be big or small, period or modern, filled with antique treasures or high-street buys; it could be a single person's pad or a bustling family house – the key is that you love it, and that you love being in it. In winter, a comfortable home is warm and cosy; in summer, it is light, bright and airy. And the secret to all this? It's decorating with your senses: sight, touch and yes, even smell and sound. Colours, patterns, shapes, styles and textures appeal to these first two senses, while the materials you choose (especially for

→ Placing a classic display inside a modern acrylic cube brings a sense of quirky irony.

↓ Fun and informal, colourful beanbags are ideal for a family home.

↓ The art and accessories you choose echo your personal sense of style.

flooring and worktops) will determine whether your home is filled with noises that are loud or soft, tinny or tinkling, high or low. Smells can be generated by creative cooking in a fabulous kitchen, deliciously scented candles or gently fragranced laundry, or something more sinister such as blocked drains or a mouldy cupboard. The way in which you design your home can influence all of these things for good or bad. It may not be obvious, but it is important. With this in mind, your decorative efforts will come together as a gorgeous, holistic whole – and all year round you will have a blissful home that has heart and soul, is calm and energising, refreshes your senses and is a joy to live in.

Span Houses
Westfield 1967–69

In the years after the Second World War, the UK experienced a mammoth housing shortage, But the local authorities' solution – impersonal prefab estates – hardly reflected the tastes of the post-war generation.

However, one innovative housing company offered a vision of brilliant designs, carefully landscaped estates and the guarantee of a friendly atmosphere. Unlike other developers of this period, who tended to focus on private domestic living, the architects behind Span (so named because it sounded fresh and modern) wanted residents to feel they were intrinsically connected with each other. Instead of driveways in front of each home, cars were kept in garages and parking areas hidden discreetly behind hedges at the rear. This forced people to walk to their homes through an open space, free of fences, where residents would interact and their children could play safely.

The driving force behind Span was maverick architect and company co-founder, Eric Lyons. He had been inspired by Walter Gropius, the leader of the influential Bauhaus design school, and especially his concept of 'group living'. Lyons worked with developer Geoffrey Townsend to create housing that combined great design with community living: an antidote to most utilitarian post-war designs.

The Westfield estate in Ashstead, Surrey, is just one of the 61 different Span estates, totalling 2,222 houses, constructed mostly in the commuter belt just outside London over the course of almost four decades. The 40 houses in Westfield were finished in 1968, and at that time 16 of them were owned by architects keen to be part of Lyons' utopian vision.

▶ The houses are protected by covenants to preserve the integrity of the estate: alterations to the front facia or windows are strictly prohibited. Paintwork must be reapplied every four years. External aerials, satellite dishes, signs and advertisements are all banned from the front of the house, along with hanging baskets or flowers.

▶ The houses in Westfield are examples of the Span K range. The houses feature wide fronts with large windows and wooden boarding, a single pitched (or sloped) roof and an angled front porch.

▶ With their steel framework, these houses have few load-bearing internal walls, so the internal layout can (and does) change. As a result these houses are customisable and somewhat open plan – a style that grew in popularity in the 1960s, as improved building techniques meant that even the smallest house could be made to feel bigger.

▶ They have large, clear windows (wooden frames with large panes) that open up the space, bringing light and the natural world into the Span home. In the upstairs back rooms the windows are placed high up on the wall in an attempt to build privacy into the estate.

▶ K style houses feature vaulted 'cathedral ceilings' in the first floor bedrooms; the ceiling helps hide the steel joints and water heater.

▶ Originally these houses would have had a sliding door between the sitting room and kitchen.

→ The houses are clad in wood with mahogany-stained, sawn wooden boarding, which acts as camouflage, blending these houses with their natural surroundings.

THE HISTORY OF THE KITCHEN p.146

CASE STUDY Clean & Colourful

This family kitchen/dining room was given the lift it needed with splashes of bright and bold colour, while maintaining clean lines and a feeling of space.

BRIEF

Richie and Anna had a young family and were gradually putting their stamp on the house they had lived in for just over two years. They loved the 1950s and 1960s aesthetic and wanted to see that reflected in their kitchen/dining room. While they were keen to retain some elements of the room, including the white units, the flooring and their designer furniture – they wanted new worktops, wall tiles, lighting and blinds. They also wanted the breakfast bar to be reduced to create more floor space. The couple expressed a preference for bold primary colours, graphic prints and crisp, clean lines, and hoped to avoid florals and animal prints.

Useful storage

Printed fabric

BEFORE

New colour scheme

→ The designer's mood board includes a beautiful watercolour image of the proposed design, as well as swatches of colour, pattern and texture.

▶ Striking blue walls contrast well with the clean, white units and soft grey worktops.

▶ New roller blinds in an eye-catching, retro print are a cost-effective choice. They make a feature of the kitchen windows, and echo the overall colour scheme.

▶ New yellow tiles echo the colour of the blinds and Richie and Anna's yellow Eiffel chairs.

▶ The breakfast bar that extended into the dining area has been cut back to give more space.

↓ Now that the breakfast bar has been reduced, the two areas of the room link together more naturally. A piece of wire between the wall and the the worktop edge provides a place to hang artwork.

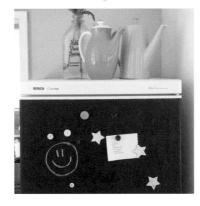

→ Blackboard paint has made the fridge a fun feature.

AFTER

↑ Adding a length of wire and some miniature pegs creates a display area for Henry's drawings and paintings.

→ The dining area is now much more stylish; the dark wall makes a feature of Richie and Anna's art.

DESIGN HIGHLIGHT

→ Plain white plates have been dipped in the paints used throughout the scheme. Lit from behind, they have become a clever wall light that co-ordinates brilliantly with the room as a whole.

→ An imaginative and inexpensive detail: plain tin cans dipped in paint and attached to the wall as vases.

←↓ Floating shelves have replaced a blocky pair of wall units to provide a generous display space above the radiator.

JUDGE'S VIEW

'The yellow and the blue-grey works really well and there are some special touches here. The dipped plates, for example, really tell the story of the colour scheme and the art wall is so sweet.'

Useful & Beautiful

Layout is key in a multi-functional space – but this family's kitchen/diner was no longer working.

BRIEF

With their family grown up, Rosie and Bruno's needs for the layout on the ground floor of their house had changed. The open-plan kitchen and dining area was a great space, but wasn't being used to its full potential: it lacked structure and the layout needed addressing. The couple wanted to remove their mismatching, freestanding units and replace them with an island that had storage, a worktop and stools so they could sit and eat there, ideally with pendant lighting above. They liked the feel of a country kitchen feel but with a modern twist, and were keen on the Shaker style with painted doors in soft colours. A window treatment for the dining area was also on their wish list.

BEFORE

Improved layout

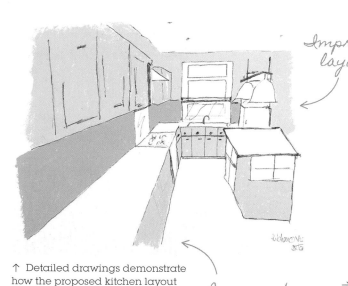

Revamped units

↑ Detailed drawings demonstrate how the proposed kitchen layout will work. The colour palette shows the designer has listened to the brief.

→ The island shown in the moodboard comes to life.

▶ The painted cupboard fronts are a modern take on traditional Shaker style. Calm and pretty, they also brighten the kitchen overall.

▶ The dated chequerboard tiles and bright red feature wall have been replaced with a painted scheme that combines soft blue, green and grey.

▶ A new 'island' unit – which is actually set against a wall – improves the room's layout and provides space for storage, food preparation and sitting and eating. It's made from an inexpensive flatpack base with a high quality wooden worktop.

▶ A new fridge unit adds more storage as well as a witty light feature.

← Jars of marmalade, illuminated from behind, make an intriguing and unusual light fitting.

↓ A pale colour scheme makes the room feel much lighter and brighter.

AFTER

→ Stick-on strips of blue film add a bright splash of colour to the windows and give a stained-glass effect.

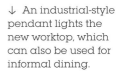

↓ An industrial-style pendant lights the new worktop, which can also be used for informal dining.

KITCHEN LAYOUTS
p.149

CASE STUDY | Out With the Old ...

These homeowners were after a complete overhaul of their kitchen and dining area, which reflected neither their taste nor the period of the house.

BRIEF

Jeff and Wendy inherited a house full of dark colours and hard finishes. Their super modern, black, high gloss kitchen was not to their taste and they were keen to introduce a softer, quirkier design. Artist Wendy and Jeff, a keen amateur baker, wanted to fuse their love of bold colour and the practicality of cooking back into their kitchen. They hoped to get rid of the high-gloss cupboards and the stainless steel-effect shutters, plinths and doors, and introduce warmth with a wooden worktop, which would complement the block wood floor. They had a preference for bright colours and bold, geometric graphics, especially from the 1950s and 1960s, and wanted their kitchen and dining area to ooze a fun and funky interior in the style of the American designer, Jonathan Adler.

BEFORE

Bold colour

Neutral walls

SOFT WALLS

· Happy Chic ·

Texture

BOLD FUN ACCESSORIES

Clean lines = No handles

1960's TEXTILES

↑ The designer's mood board is a collage of pattern, colour, images and words.

Fun accessories

→ White cupboard fronts really lift the feel of the room.

▶ The fresh white walls echo the newly painted cupboard doors, making the room light, bright and airy.

▶ The new wooden worktops feel warm and welcoming; they also complement the original woodblock flooring.

▶ Colour has been introduced with new artwork, quirky accessories and striped pelmets above the kitchen and dining room windows. The new scheme, in green, orange and yellow, complements Jeff and Wendy's existing table and chairs.

▶ Chunky shelves have replaced the wall units, making the room feel more open and informal. They hold good-looking displays of retro crockery.

AFTER

DESIGN HIGHLIGHT

↓ This well-thought out display provides an eye-catching feature on a large, plain wall.

↓ Small touches of colour add interest to a room that is clean, bright and functional.

↓ Similar to the wall display, this group of items reflects the homeowners' style and adds colour to the room.

← The thoughtful touch of a brightly coloured flex ties this simple pendant in with the overall scheme.

JUDGE'S VIEW

'The group of retro fabrics in coloured frames on the wall are really nice. With a mixture of square and rectangular shapes, in a range of sizes, it's quite graphic.'

Project

The designers at Westfield were each given three white porcelain plates to incorporate into their design. It's quick and easy to decorate your own plate using special ceramic paints.

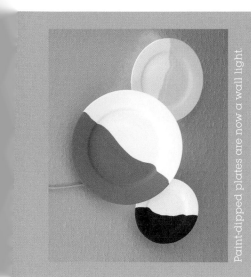

Paint-dipped plates are now a wall light

Glued-on mugs make a clever cake stand

Smashed plates create a 1960s-style mosaic

HOW TO PAINT PORCELAIN PLATES

1 First make sure your plate is clean, dry and free from dust. Make a template of the design to fit your plate and lay it on top of a piece of transfer paper. Use sticky tape to fix it to the plate and trace the design with a ballpoint pen. When you remove the transfer paper your design will be visible on the plate.

2 Using porcelain paint (food-safe if you are going to use the plates for eating), mix your paint colour, and apply directly to the plate. You can use paint pens, a brush, or put your mixed paint in an applicator bottle.

3 Allow the paint to dry for two hours and then use a baby wipe to remove the transfer lines. Place on a baking tray and heat in the oven for 30 minutes at 150ºC/300ºF/Gas Mark 2. Remove from the oven and allow to cool.

DISPLAYS ON WALLS p.222

Judges' top 5 tips

Sophie

Interior stylist Sophie runs her own interior design business and works regularly as a writer and stylist for interiors and design magazines. She has also appeared on BBC, ITV and Channel 5.

▶ A window is to a view what a frame is to a painting, so don't scrimp on them. I love combing curtains and blinds in co-ordinating fabrics for the ultimate well-dressed look. To maximise the amount of natural light in your room, make sure the curtain pole or track exceeds the width of the window, so that curtains can be drawn all the way clear of the window panes.

▶ Creating a feature wall involves wallpapering one wall in a room in a bold arresting print; it is a great way to introduce pattern and colour into your scheme, while also being affordable. Think about situating the feature paper on the wall behind a bed or sofa: this way it can add visual interest to a room without having to look at it while you are relaxing.

▶ Avoid using pure white on your walls: in the Northern Hemisphere daylight already has a lot of blue in it, so bright white can make rooms feel cold and dingy. Instead choose an off white with a warm tint to it – often called 'Old White', 'Linen White' or, dare I say it, 'Magnolia'. Grey is big in interiors at the moment and my tip is to go for a warmer shade of grey and avoid cool blue-greys unless your room is bursting with sunshine.

▶ Hard floors are increasingly popular as they're hardwearing, easy to clean and great for people with allergies. If you can't afford a spectacular rug, consider getting a carpet remnant whipped around the edges. Wool rugs feel nicer and last longer, but polypropylene is best for dealing with spills, and so is a good choice for family or childrens' rooms.

▶ The colour you choose can have a huge impact on the feel of a room. Typically cool colours, such as blue, lilac, green and grey make a room feel larger. Cosy colours, such as red, yellow and orange, work to make the space feel smaller.

← Feature walls in bedrooms are a good way to express your personality.

Daniel

Dan trained and worked as an architect before setting up his own interior design company. As well as being a writer and television presenter, he is also involved with professional development at the British Institute of Interior Design and the KLC School of Design.

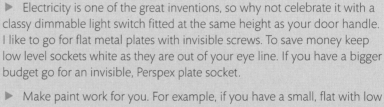

▶ Electricity is one of the great inventions, so why not celebrate it with a classy dimmable light switch fitted at the same height as your door handle. I like to go for flat metal plates with invisible screws. To save money keep low level sockets white as they are out of your eye line. If you have a bigger budget go for an invisible, Perspex plate socket.

▶ Make paint work for you. For example, if you have a small, flat with low ceilings, paint the hallway dark. Then, when you enter one of your main rooms, it will feel so much more light and airy. Paint your bedroom in warm tones so that without your clothes you will look even more fabulous.

▶ Many people, Sophie included, are very keen on cushions, but my advice is to show a little restraint. I believe successful design should look natural and unaffected. Therefore, if you do have a cushion fetish, do something different like piling them high; don't put them at an angle – always keep horizontal to the seat cushion.

▶ Design democracy at home can lead to beige rooms. Instead, designate a decision maker for each room according to who uses it the most. The result will be that your home will have more personality and rooms will be happy spaces for those that use them the most.

▶ MDF is a wonder material and even the most expensive of high street kitchens don't have the privilege of being made from it. It is maligned as a cheap material but it isn't, it is how it is handled that makes a difference. For example, cut edges need to be addressed as the grain will expand if painted. Edge with painter's tape or batten. Try staining raw MDF: there is something very cool and modern about the finish.

← Celebrate the invention of electricity with unusual light fittings.

Further information

Presenter profiles

Tom Dyckhoff

'Architecture and Design doesn't have to be unapproachable - interior design is something that we can all do to connect to our homes and reflect our character.'

Tom has written widely for publications from *The Sunday Telegraph* to *GQ*. He's the architecture and design critic of *The Times* newspaper and has written the weekly 'Let's Move To ...' column for *The Guardian Weekend* magazine for more than a decade.

He appears regularly as a critic on TV and radio programmes: in 2009, his seven-part BBC Two series, *Saving Britain's Past* examined Britain's obsession with heritage. Other television credits include *The Culture Show* and *The Secret Life of Buildings*.

Sophie Robinson

'You don't have to go into posh houses to see beautiful interiors; you can find them in the most unexpected homes in Britain.'

Sophie Robinson has been in the interior design business for over 15 years, earning the reputation as one of the industry's top interior stylists. After studying furniture design at university Sophie went on to produce her own range of lighting for Liberty. She then moved into journalism, becoming Home Editor for BBC *GoodHomes* magazine.

Since setting up her own business she has continued to write for a number of interiors magazines such as *House Beautiful*, *Livingetc* and *Ideal Home*. She has also appeared on BBC, ITV and Channel 5.

Daniel Hopwood

'You can't learn about interior design, it has to be in your soul as a passion – passion that comes from going around stately homes at the age of six and loving it, or nicking your sister's dolls house and playing with it.'

After training and working as an architect, Daniel set up his own interior design company in 1993. Outside his office work he is Director of Continuing Professional Development at the British Institute of Interior Design as well as its Vice President. He is also a guest tutor at the KLC School of Design.

A former trends consultant and design writer, Daniel has also presented Channel 4's *Britain's Best Homes*.

The Great Interior Design Challenge featured some leading names in British architecture and interior design.

Contestant profiles

Jane Beale

'I have been told I have a talent for creating a luxurious, polished but homely look.' Mum and part-time events co-ordinator Jane from Kent, likes to use colour, texture and accessories to create living spaces that are inviting and stylish as well as functional.

Helen Bottrill

'If I can't find what I want, I make it, it's easy.' Helen lives in Devon and designs and creates bespoke textiles from her collection of bold fabrics. Her style is a mismatching mix of the old and the new and she believes that everyone's home should reflect their personality.

Dee Cartwright

'Interiors is not what I do anymore ... it's who I am now.' Dee is a housewife from Kent who believes that interior design should make someone feel that their space is utterly personal to them. Her style is New England meets English country.

Jordan Cluroe

'I'd absolutely love to be an interior designer ... I think I'd be quite good.' A coffee-shop owner from London, Jordan has renovated several properties and loves all aspects of interior design. He believes in good design, but thinks functionality is just as important.

Alice Davies

'I love the transformative feeling of well-being a really beautifully designed space can offer and all the compliments I receive when I have visitors!' Full-time mum Alice from East Sussex has an adventurous spirit when it comes to design, and likes using strong colours.

Jenny Elesmore

'A nice home is one where you sit down and say "ahhh".' Jenny owns a lifestyle shop in Cornwall. She believes homes don't have to be over complicated by style and you can achieve a great look with a little imagination. Her style is traditional with a modern twist.

Paula Holland

'I love taking an unloved, neglected space and making it liveable again.' Paula is a pub landlady in Herefordshire and has renovated a number of properties including her pub, which has two Bed & Breakfast rooms. Her style is homely and comfortable.

Lynne Lambourne

'It started aged seven ... when I was re-arranging my bedroom.' Based in Buckinghamshire, Lynne runs her own children's fashion business. Her style is 'Scandi-chic' and she believes that everyone can make their home feel different with a little time and effort.

Julia Matthews

'I have a great eye for detail and can capture the qualities of a room.' A commercialisation co-ordinator from Nottingham, Julia also runs her own business that creates artwork out of children's handprints. She describes her style is minimalist but homely.

Louise Rummery

'I am unable to walk into someone's house and not check out what they have (or usually haven't) done to the space.' An executive assistant from Hampshire, Louise describes her style as bold and dramatic, masculine but with a feminine touch.

Lorna Satchell

'Interior design is about not being afraid and saying, "Actually I like this and this is how I want to display it".' Lorna from Birmingham is passionate about blending modern and traditional styles and prides herself on being frugal and thrifty.

Amy Tollafield

'I don't want to chase trends; I have my own spin on things.' Born in Cornwall but now based in Somerset, freelance artist Amy also runs a small business selling items she makes out of driftwood. Her design style is bohemian and coastal.

Emma Chapman

'...like David Bowie; I don't ...ck to one era or style.' A ...red optician from London, ...na believes she has always ...d an interest in interiors. Her ...le is always evolving and ...e likes to have the flexibility ...change a room every ...w years.

Helen Charlton

'Your home has to feel relaxed with treasures around you, each with their own story.' Helen is a part-time teacher from Durham who also runs her own craft business. Her French farmhouse-style home has featured in several publications including *Country Homes & Interiors*.

Johnny China

'What I love about interior design is creating something that has personality.' Currently based in Devon, painter and decorator Johnny is interested in all aspects of design and has a retro eclectic style. He is now retraining and hopes to pursue a career in interiors.

Susan Garrett

'...don't like to follow trends; I like ...be unique.' With five children ...nd four grandchildren, Susan ...om Kent has dedicated her ...e to her family, but has always ...njoyed designing her home. ...er style is colourful and she ...es interesting rooms in which ...eople can discover things.

Neil Gaukwin

'I do get an enjoyable feeling from looking at a space that I've created.' Neil from East Sussex loves experimenting with second-hand items: his style is 'updated granny chic'. A creative by trade, he likes to take ordinary objects and reuse them in new ways.

James Gostelow

'I'm very English and thrive off British designers.' An asset manager from Surrey, James says he lives and breathes interiors and never fully switches off. His style is ultimately traditional with a modern edge and he believes it is integral to be true to the property's period.

Emma McDonald

'...make vintage doll's houses ...o stop me changing my own!' ...A self-employed vintage ...homeware and craft dealer ...rom Manchester, Emma ...as her own blog and has ...esigned 11 homes according ...o her evolving style, which is ...urrently modern retro chic.

Sarah Moore

'I buy second hand and old furniture and give it a new lease of life.' Sarah from West Sussex trained as a chef and worked in catering before starting an online vintage shop and writing about vintage style. She favours a colourful and eclectic vintage look.

Kimberly Plested

'I hate clichés but interior design is my life.' A mum and student from Oxfordshire, Kimberly is now pursuing her childhood dream of studying interior design. With a simple and natural style she loves bringing unique ideas to life.

Nigel Tooze

'...ve always been obsessed ...ith interiors – now I'm taking ...giant leap and want to make ...career out of it.' Nigel from ...ondon is taking time off from ...is work as a financial lawyer ...o explore the possibility of ...orking as an interior designer. ...is style is classical theatrical.

Luke Watkins

'My talent lies in being able to understand someone else's taste quickly.' A sales assistant in Oxfordshire, Luke studied interior and spatial design and has worked in the building trade. He describes his style as 'rustic meets modern', and likes skip and loft rummage finds.

Charmaine White

'I eat sleep and breathe everything interior design.' A design student from London, with a background in retail Charmaine believes interior designing is about taking people outside of their comfort zones. Her style is sophisticated, chic and modern.

The contestants on *The Great Interior Design Challenge* showed a wide range of design styles and a variety of different talents.

Directory

DIY

B&Q
Everything for DIY.
0845 609 6688
www.diy.com

Brewers
A wide range of decorating materials.
0845 504 5040
www.brewers.co.uk for branches

Buildbase
Builders merchants.
www.buildbase.co.uk for branches

Hobbycraft
The UK's leading art and craft retailer.
0330 026 1400
www.hobbycraft.co.uk

Homebase
Decorating and DIY.
0845 077 8888
www.homebase.co.uk

Jewson
Sustainable timber and building materials.
www.jewson.co.uk for branches

Screwfix
Trade tools, plumbing, electrical, bathrooms and kitchens.
0500 414141
www.screwfix.com

Wickes
Value-for-money home improvement and the building trade.
0370 218 6327
www.wickes.co.uk

Paint

Crown
One of the UK's largest paint manufacturers.
www.crownpaint.co.uk

Dulux
Huge range of household paints.
www.dulux.co.uk

Earthborn
Stylish, high performance paints that are safer to use and sound for the environment.
01928 734171 for stockists
www.earthbornpaints.co.uk

Little Greene
Quality paints with great depth of colour and coverage.
0845 880 5855
www.littlegreene.com

Farrow & Ball
Unrivalled paint colours made using the finest ingredients and age-old methods.
01202 876141
www.farrow-ball.com

One-stop shops

Argos
Huge range of value furnishings, homeware and accessories.
0845 640 3030
www.argos.co.uk for branches

BhS
Fashionable looks for your home.
www.bhs.co.uk for branches

Cargo
Great value, stylish homewares and furnishings.
0844 848 3300
www.cargohomeshop.com

The Conran Shop
Beautifully designed furniture, lighting, accessories and gifts.
0844 848 4000 for branches
www.conran.com

Debenhams
Department store with a strong range of designer brands.
08445 616161 for branches
www.debenhams.com

Dunelm Mill
Leading home furnishing retailer.
0845 1656565
www.dunelm-mill.com

HomeSense
Designer homewares at up to 60% off.
01923 473 000 for branches
www.homesense.com

House of Fraser
Leading department store.
0845 602 1073
www.houseoffraser.co.uk

Ikea
Affordable solutions for better living.
www.ikea.com for worldwide stores

John Lewis
Everything for the home; never knowingly undersold.
08456 049 049
www.johnlewis.com

Laura Ashley
Much-loved traditional home furnishings.
0871 983 5999
www.lauraashley.com

Marks & Spencer
0845 302 1234
www.marksandspencer.com
Leading British retailer.

Muji
'No brand' quality furniture and accessories.
www.muji.eu for branches

Next
Homewares with style, quality and value for money.
0844 844 8939
www.next.co.uk

Sainsbury's
Homewares and accessories from a leading supermarket.
www.sainsburys.co.uk for branches

Selfridges
Stylish department store with great homewares.
0800 123 400 for branches
www.selfridges.com

Tesco Direct
Huge supermarket with a wide range of products.
0800 323 4050
www.tesco.com/direct

Very
Digital department store.
08448 222 321
www.very.co.uk

World Stores
Everything for the home and garden, online.
0844 931 1005
www.worldstores.co.uk

Decorating

Abode Interiors
Designer furniture and glass coffee tables.
0116 2600 252
www.abode-interiors.co.uk

Atelier Abigail Ahern
Quirky, cool statement pieces.
020 7354 8181
www.atelierabigailahern.com

Bombay Duck
Discovering the fabulous in the everyday.
020 8749 3000
www.bombayduck.co.uk

Bathstore
Stylish bathroom products at a good price.
www.bathstore.com for branches

Brume
Made to measure window film.
01364 73090
www.brume.co.uk

Carpet Right
Contemporary and traditional flooring.
0845 604 5593
www.carpetright.co.uk

Cath Kidston
Witty, reworked English country-house style.
08450 262 440 for branches
www.cathkidston.co.uk

The Contemporary Home
Eclectic interiors products.
02392 469400
www.tch.net

Cox & Cox
Unusual, beautiful and
practical products by mail
order.
0844 858 0734
www.coxandcox.co.uk

The Curtain Factory Outlet
Curtaining and upholstery
fabrics, ready-made curtains
and accessories.
020 8492 0093
www.curtainfactoryoutlet.co.uk

Designers Guild
Creative, colourful furnishing
fabrics, wallcoverings,
upholstery and bed and bath
collections.
www.designersguild.com for
branches

Etsy
Worldwide marketplace
for hand-made and unique
goods.
www.etsy.com

Fired Earth
An exclusive collection
of wall tiles, floor tiles,
designer paints, kitchens and
bathrooms.
0845 293 8798
www.firedearth.com

Flooring Supplies
The UK's largest online
flooring company.
0800 999 8100
www.flooringsupplies.co.uk

Graham & Green
Global, glamorous and
gorgeous furniture, lighting
and accessories.
020 7243 8908/020 7586
2960
www.grahamandgreen.co.uk

Greengate
Nostalgic and pretty
patterned homeware.
www.int.greengate.dk for
stores

Habitat
Affordable, functional
modern design.

www.habitat.net for stores

Harlequin
Classic-meets-contemporary
prints, weaves and
wallcoverings.
www.harlequin.uk.com

Ian Mankin
Natural and organic fabrics,
woven in the UK.
020 7722 0997
www.ianmankin.co.uk

Labour & Wait
Timeless, functional products
for everyday life.
020 7729 6253
www.labourandwait.co.uk

Liberty
Quintessential English
emporium.
020 7734 1234
www.liberty.co.uk

Melin Tregwynt
Traditional Welsh weaving
combined with innovative,
modern design.
01348 891288/02920 224997
www.melintregwynt.co.uk

Not on the High Street
Original items from creative
small businesses.
0845 259 1359
www.notonthehighstreet.com

Online Carpets
Inexpensive carpets and vinyl
flooring.
0800 9705 705
www.onlinecarpets.co.uk

Roger Oates
Classic wool flatweave rugs
and runners.
01531 632718 for stockists
www.rogeroates.com

Sanderson
Quintessentially English
fabrics and wallpapers, bed
linen, paint and tableware
collections.
www.sanderson-uk.com

Scion
Refreshing new British
furnishings brand.
www.scion.uk.com

Sofa.com
Comfy, quality sofas,

armchairs and beds.
0845 400 2222
www.sofa.com

SofaSofa
Quality sofas direct from the
manufacturers.
01495 244226
www.sofasofa.co.uk

Solid Surface Kitchens Direct
Ready-made worksurfaces,
kitchens and kitchen
accessories from industry
leaders at some of the
cheapest prices available.
0845 269 7517
www.solidsurfacekitchens.
co.uk/

Store
One-stop shop for your
storage needs.
0844 414 2885
www.aplaceforeverything.
co.uk

Toast
Laid-back linens, crockery
and accessories.
0844 557 0460 for branches
www.toast.co.uk

Topps Tiles
The UK's biggest tile and
wood flooring specialist.
0800 783 6262
www.toppstiles.co.uk

The White Company
Stylish, affordable, designer-
quality linens and accessories.
0845 678 8150 for branches
www.thewhitecompany.com

Worktop Express
Leading online solid wood
worktop specialist.
0845 2222644
www.worktop-express.co.uk

Zazous
An online shop with original,
design-led items.
01843 602800
www.zazous.co.uk

Wallpaper Direct
Enormous choice of
wallpapers.
01323 430886
www.wallpaperdirect.com

Second-hand, recycled & vintage

After Noah
Unusual and interesting
antiques, vintage and
contemporary furnishings.
020 7359 4281
www.afternoah.com

Baileys
A mix of vintage and new
that's integral to a repair, reuse and rethink philosophy.
01989 561931
www.baileyshomeandgarden.
com

Bubbledrum
Vintage industrial, reclaimed
and hand-made items.
020 3092 8974
www.bubbledrum.co.uk

LassCo
Prime resource for
architectural antiques, salvage
and curiosities.
020 7749 9944
www.lassco.co.uk

Masco Salvage
Reclaimed architectural
features and traditional
building materials.
01285 760886
www.mascosalvage.com

Re
A fab mix of pieces that are
rare, remarkable, recycled and
restored.
01434 634567
www.re-foundobjects.com

Retropolitan
Stylish and affordable
decorative vintage homeware.
07870 422182
www.retropolitan.co.uk

Salvo
Gateway to the world of
architectural salvage and
antiques.
www.salvoweb.com

Winter's Moon
A quirky assortment
of vintage, recycled
or handmade furniture and
home accessories.
07783 768503
www.wintersmoon.co.uk

Index